INTRODUCING ISSUES WITH OPPOSING VIEWPOINTS®

3/11/09

Rap Music

Noël Merino, *Book Editor*

GREENHAVEN PRESS
A part of Gale, Cengage Learning

GALE
CENGAGE Learning™

Detroit • New York • San Francisco • New Haven, Conn • Waterville, Maine • London

Christine Nasso, *Publisher*
Elizabeth Des Chenes, *Managing Editor*

For more information, contact:
Greenhaven Press
27500 Drake Rd.
Farmington Hills, MI 48331-3535
Or you can visit our Internet site at gale.cengage.com

For product information and technology assistance, contact us at

Gale Customer Support, 1-800-877-4253
For permission to use material from this text or product, submit all requests online at www.cengage.com/permissions

Further permissions questions can be emailed to permissionrequest@cengage.com

Articles in Greenhaven Press anthologies are often edited for length to meet page requirements. In addition, original titles of these works are changed to clearly present the main thesis and to explicitly indicate the author's opinion. Every effort is made to ensure that Greenhaven Press accurately reflects the original intent of the authors. Every effort has been made to trace the owners of copyrighted material.

Cover image copyright Arman Zhenikeyev, 2008. Used under license from Shutterstock.com

LIBRARY OF CONGRESS CATALOGING-IN-PUBLICATION DATA

Rap music / Noël Merino, book editor.
   p. cm. — (Introducing issues with opposing viewpoints)
Includes bibliographical references (p.   ) and index.
ISBN-13: 978-0-7377-3978-7 (hardcover) 1. Rap (Music)—Social aspects. I. Merino, Noël.
ML3918.R37R36 2008
306.4'84249—dc22

                                                                                              2008002105

Printed in the United States of America
1 2 3 4 5 6 7 12 11 10 09 08

Contents

Chapter 3: Does Rap Music Promote Violence?

Foreword

I ndulging in a wide spectrum of ideas, beliefs, and perspectives is a critical cornerstone of democracy. After all, it is often debates over differences of opinion, such as whether to legalize abortion, how to treat prisoners, or when to enact the death penalty, that shape our society and drive it forward. Such diversity of thought is frequently regarded as the hallmark of a healthy and civilized culture. As the Reverend Clifford Schutjer of the First Congregational Church in Mansfield, Ohio, declared in a 2001 sermon, "Surrounding oneself with only like-minded people, restricting what we listen to or read only to what we find agreeable is irresponsible. Refusing to entertain doubts once we make up our minds is a subtle but deadly form of arrogance." With this advice in mind, Introducing Issues with Opposing Viewpoints books aim to open readers' minds to the critically divergent views that comprise our world's most important debates.

Introducing Issues with Opposing Viewpoints simplifies for students the enormous and often overwhelming mass of material now available via print and electronic media. Collected in every volume is an array of opinions that captures the essence of a particular controversy or topic. Introducing Issues with Opposing Viewpoints books embody the spirit of nineteenth-century journalist Charles A. Dana's axiom: "Fight for your opinions, but do not believe that they contain the whole truth, or the only truth." Absorbing such contrasting opinions teaches students to analyze the strength of an argument and compare it to its opposition. From this process readers can inform and strengthen their own opinions, or be exposed to new information that will change their minds. Introducing Issues with Opposing Viewpoints is a mosaic of different voices. The authors are statesmen, pundits, academics, journalists, corporations, and ordinary people who have felt compelled to share their experiences and ideas in a public forum. Their words have been collected from newspapers, journals, books, speeches, interviews, and the Internet, the fastest growing body of opinionated material in the world.

Introducing Issues with Opposing Viewpoints shares many of the well-known features of its critically acclaimed parent series, Opposing Viewpoints. The articles are presented in a pro/con format, allowing readers to absorb divergent perspectives side by side. Active reading questions preface each viewpoint, requiring the student to approach the material thoughtfully and carefully. Useful charts, graphs, and cartoons supplement each article. A thorough introduction provides readers with crucial background on an issue. An annotated bibliography points the reader toward articles, books, and Web sites that contain additional information on the topic. An appendix of organizations to contact contains a wide variety of charities, nonprofit organizations, political groups, and private enterprises that each hold a position on the issue at hand. Finally, a comprehensive index allows readers to locate content quickly and efficiently.

Introducing Issues with Opposing Viewpoints is also significantly different from Opposing Viewpoints. As the series title implies, its presentation will help introduce students to the concept of opposing viewpoints and learn to use this material to aid in critical writing and debate. The series' four-color, accessible format makes the books attractive and inviting to readers of all levels. In addition, each viewpoint has been carefully edited to maximize a reader's understanding of the content. Short but thorough viewpoints capture the essence of an argument. A substantial, thought-provoking essay question placed at the end of each viewpoint asks the student to further investigate the issues raised in the viewpoint, compare and contrast two authors' arguments, or consider how one might go about forming an opinion on the topic at hand. Each viewpoint contains sidebars that include at-a-glance information and handy statistics. A Facts About section located in the back of the book further supplies students with relevant facts and figures.

Following in the tradition of the Opposing Viewpoints series, Greenhaven Press continues to provide readers with invaluable exposure to the controversial issues that shape our world. As John Stuart Mill once wrote: "The only way in which a human being can make some approach to knowing the whole of a subject is by hearing what can be said about it by persons of every variety of opinion and studying all modes in which it can be looked at by every character of mind. No wise man ever acquired his wisdom in any mode but this." It is to this principle that Introducing Issues with Opposing Viewpoints books are dedicated.

Introduction

"So who gets to say 'ho,' in an age when Pimp My Ride *is an innocent car show and* It's Hard Out Here for a Pimp *is an Oscar-winning song?"*

—James Poniewozik, media critic

Rap music has been a source of controversy since it entered mainstream popularity in the United States during the 1980s. The emergence of the genre known as "gangsta rap" in the 1990s intensified this debate, as the music contained explicit lyrics about violence, sex, misogyny, and drugs. This debate was brought into mainstream discussion in the spring of 2007, after comments made by Don Imus, "shock jock" radio host of *Imus in the Morning.*

During his radio show on April 9, 2007, Imus was discussing the NCAA Women's Basketball Championship. During this discussion, he referred to the members of the Rutgers University women's basketball team (which is comprised of eight African American women and two Caucasian women) as "nappy-headed hos." He apologized for the remarks the next day and, shortly thereafter, was fired from his job and his show was cancelled. On NBC's *Today* show, he noted that he did not invent the derogatory language, stating that it had "originated in the black community." This was the beginning of a debate about the use of similar language within rap music lyrics, videos, and popular culture.

The treatment of Imus after his comment caused many people to question why people were so outraged at Imus when language of the sort he used is heard frequently in rap music. Columnist and political commentator Michelle Malkin asked, "You know, what Imus said, isn't it a drop in the ocean compared to the filth on music and radio and hip-hop stations every day in this country?" Many echo Malkin's sentiment, wondering why it is fine for rap musicians to use this language but, when used by a radio personality, is grounds for being fired. Political analyst Pat Buchanan believes that part of the reason Imus was fired was because of his race: "If Don Imus had been black, nothing would have been done to him. As we're hearing right here, it's the very fact he was white and his insulting comment was made about black women."

While the outrage over Imus's comments led some to question why Imus was being treated harshly compared to rap music stars, others took the opportunity to reiterate their outrage at the use of certain language, whether by Imus or in rap music. Dr. E. Faye Williams, speaking on behalf of the National Congress of Black Women (NCBW) argues, "Don Imus was wrong when he belittled the young women at Rutgers. . . . [Knicks coach] Isiah Thomas is wrong when he says that it's highly offensive for a white male to call a Black female a bitch, but it's okay for a Black man to do so. Well, Mr. Thomas would be surprised to know that they're equally offensive and totally unacceptable to Black women."

While outrage over the lyrics found in rap music is commonplace, there is no consensus on what to do about the situation. In response to the debate emerging after the Imus incident, Russell Simmons and Dr. Benjamin Chavis made a statement on behalf of the Hip-Hop Summit Action Network (HSAN) recommending "that the recording and broadcast industries voluntarily remove/bleep/delete the misogynistic words 'bitch' and 'ho' and the racially offensive word 'nigger.'" While this recommendation calls for voluntary censorship, some go farther in wanting more government regulation. Arguing that freedom of speech needs to be tempered with responsibility for not causing harm, the NCBW claims, "Yes, rights without responsibilities should be labeled anarchy; yet that is much of what we see and hear on our public airwaves. It's time for Congress to stand up and insist upon responsibility, and make it clear to the FCC [Federal Communications Commission] and the FTC [Federal Trade Commission] what their roles should be in making it happen." The concern here is largely about the content of public airwaves—the same public airwaves where Imus made his comments.

The focus on music lyrics is of concern to many. Media expert Shelly Palmer worries that focusing on the lyrics of rap music is not going to fix any problems: "If you want to fix rap lyrics, fix the society it reflects. Would you try to fix blues lyrics because they depict a sad and cruel world? Would you try to fix or change country lyrics because they depict the trials and tribulations of life in rural America? Of course not. Rap, like all art, is a mirror." Others are concerned about any censorship of lyrics, wanting rap music to be given the same First Amendment protection as any other artwork: "Mark Twain's literary classic, *Huckleberry Finn*, is still required reading in classrooms across the United States of America. The word 'nigger' appears in the book approximately 215 times. While some may find this offensive, the book was not banned by all school districts because of its artistic value. The same consideration should be extended to hip-hop music." While broad censorship is an unlikely result, people are unlikely to agree upon just what, if anything, should be done about rap music. *Introducing Issues with Opposing Viewpoints: Rap Music* explores a variety of viewpoints on the various debates about rap music, such as this one.

Chapter 1

How Does Rap Music Impact Culture?

Since rap music began, people have questioned the role its lyrics have played in urban culture.

Viewpoint

1

Rap Music Reflects a Deeper Problem with Black Culture

Thomas Chatterton Williams

"Hip-hop culture is not black culture, it's black street culture."

In the following viewpoint Thomas Chatterton Williams argues that while the popular media has focused much energy on whether rap music, or hip-hop, has a negative effect on society, the real concern is deeper than the music. Williams claims that the glorification of "black street culture" in rap music is a problem that goes beyond the music itself—black culture, Williams argues, needs to be disentangled from the black street culture glorified by rap music. Williams is a graduate student in the Cultural Reporting and Criticism program at New York University.

AS YOU READ, CONSIDER THE FOLLOWING QUESTIONS:
1. Since the late 1970s, where has black America received its values, aesthetic sensibility, and self-image, according to the author?

2. What analogy does the author make regarding Chinese Americans to illustrate the point that most Americans do not want to "class sink"?
3. What does the author say happens to black students who have a GPA of 3.5 and above?

O ver the past three decades black culture has grown so conflated with hip-hop culture that for most Americans under the age of 45, hip-hop culture is black culture. Except that it's not. During the controversy over Don Imus's comments this spring [2007], the radio host was pilloried for using the same sexist language that is condoned, if not celebrated, in hip-hop music and culture. As the scandal evolved, some critics, including the Rev. Al Sharpton and the NAACP, shifted their attention to the rap industry. Indeed, every couple of years, it seems, we ask ourselves: Is hip-hop poisonous? Is it misogynistic, violent and nihilistic? What kind of message is it sending?

FAST FACT

While some people use the terms "rap" and "hip-hop" interchangeably, rap music is usually considered only one part of hip-hop culture, which is a combination of rapping, DJing, breakdancing, and graffiti art.

Black Culture in Trouble

But what critics consistently fail to emphasize in these sporadic storms of opprobrium, as most did during the Imus affair, is that the stakes transcend hip-hop: Black culture itself is in trouble.

Born in the projects of the South Bronx, tweaked to its gangsta form in the 'hoods of South Central Los Angeles and dumbed down unconscionably in the ghettos of the "Dirty South" (the original Confederate states, minus Missouri and Kentucky), there are no two ways about it—hip-hop culture is not black culture, it's black street culture. Despite 40 years of progress since the civil rights movement, in the hip-hop era—from the late 1970s onward—black America, uniquely, began receiving its values, aesthetic sensibility and self-image almost entirely from the street up.

This is a major departure for blacks, who traditionally saw cultivation as a key to equality. Think of the days when W.E.B. Du Bois "[sat] with Shakespeare" and moved "arm in arm with Balzac;" or when Ralph Ellison waxed universal and spoke of the need "to extend one's humanity and one's knowledge of human life."

Some people claim that rap music has glorified a "street culture" that is not common to all blacks.

Glorifying the Lower Class

The historian Paul Fussell notes that for most Americans, it is difficult to "class sink." Try to imagine the Chinese American son of oncologists—living in, say, a New York suburb such as Westchester, attending private school—who feels subconsciously compelled to model his life, even if only superficially, on that of a Chinese mafioso dealing heroin on the Lower East Side. The cultural pressure for a middle-class Chinese American to walk, talk and act like a lower-class thug from Chinatown is nil. The same can be said of Jews, or of any other ethnic group.

But in black America the folly is so commonplace it fails to attract serious attention. Like neurotics obsessed with amputating their own healthy limbs, middle-class blacks concerned with "keeping it real" are engaging in gratuitously self-destructive and violently masochistic behavior.

Sociologists have a term for this pathological facet of black life. It's called "cool-pose culture." Whatever the nomenclature, "cool pose" or keeping it real or something else entirely, this peculiar aspect of the contemporary black experience—the inverted-pyramid hierarchy of values stemming from the glorification of lower-class reality in the hip-hop era—has quietly taken the place of white racism as the most formidable obstacle to success and equality in the black middle classes.

The Price of Romanticizing Street Culture

As John H. McWhorter emphasizes in his book *Losing the Race: Self-Sabotage in Black America,* "forty years after the Civil Rights Act, African-American students on the average are the weakest in the United States, at all ages, in all subjects, and regardless of class level." Reading and math proficiency test results consistently show this. Clearly, this *nostalgie de la boue,* this longing for the mud, exacts a hefty price.

A 2005 study by Roland G. Fryer of Harvard University crystallizes the point: While there is scarce dissimilarity in popularity levels among low-achieving students, black or white, Fryer finds that "when a student achieves a 2.5 GPA, clear differences start to emerge." At

3.5 and above, black students "tend to have fewer and fewer friends," even as their high-achieving white peers "are at the top of the popularity pyramid." With such pressure to be real, to not "act white," is it any wonder that the African American high school graduation rate has stagnated at 70 percent for the past three decades?

Until black culture as a whole is effectively disentangled from the python-grip of hip-hop, and by extension the street, we are not going to see any real progress.

EVALUATING THE AUTHOR'S ARGUMENTS:

Williams argues that rap music, as part of hip-hop culture, glorifies black street culture. Such glorification, he says, has many negative effects for the black community in society. Do you agree that rap music glorifies black street culture? How do you think rap artists would answer this assertion?

Rap Music Can Be a Positive Force of Black Culture

Alexandra Marks

"The industry has a responsibility to counter the glorification of guns and street hustling with a realistic message that empowers kids. . . ."

Alexandra Marks argues in the following viewpoint that the hip-hop industry can use its power to positively transform black culture rather than continue producing music that incites violence. Alexandra Marks is a staff writer for the *Christian Science Monitor*.

AS YOU READ, CONSIDER THE FOLLOWING QUESTIONS:
1. What conviction does the author claim "amounts to heresy" in parts of the rap world?
2. What components comprise the "peace project" developed by the National Hip-Hop Summit Youth Council?
3. According to Marks, why have some academics cautioned against condemning rap lyrics?

With the kind of in-your-face boast common to the hard-edge beats of hip-hop, rapper Jay-Z rhymes out in a recent video: "No matter how much money I got, I'm still gonna sell rock, on the block."

Translated, he's still going to deal drugs in the neighborhood.

But youth activist Pee Wee Kirkland is determined that young kids see the truth in that artistic invention.

"You got to tell them selling drugs is against the law. Selling drugs, there's a consequence," he says. "And then you got to explain to them that Jay-Z ain't in Brooklyn selling drugs. He's in the [mostly white, exclusive] Hamptons."

Mr. Kirkland, himself a former gangster and drug dealer, is part of a nascent reform movement spearheaded by some of the biggest names in rap. Called Hip-Hop 4 Peace, it's determined to use the power of the industry to reduce the violence and change the face of the controversial genre. It was launched this week [November 10, 2002] in New York by LL Cool J's former manager Charles Fisher and Grammy award-winning artist Chuck D.

At the core of their campaign is a conviction that amounts to heresy in some quarters of the rap world: that artistic images do influence behavior, especially when it comes to young people, and that the industry has a responsibility to counter the glorification of guns and street hustling with a realistic message that empowers kids, rather than landing them in jail.

Rap Artists Fight Back

The campaign is part of a larger transformation under way in the hip-hop world, which emerged from the ghetto in New York more than a quarter century ago. While the media has focused primarily on the violent lyrics and images, particularly in so-called "gangsta rap," many other artists have been developing a social critique and nurturing hip-hop's potential political power to deal with issues from education funding to gun control.

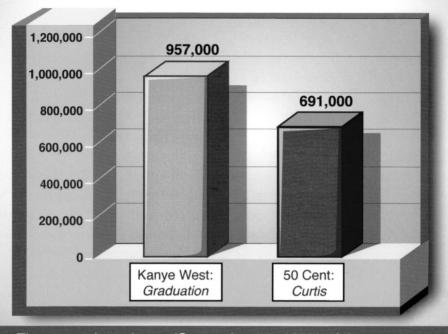

First Week Album Sales: Kanye West v. 50 Cent

957,000

691,000

| 1,200,000 |
| 1,000,000 |
| 800,000 |
| 600,000 |
| 400,000 |
| 200,000 |
| 0 |

Kanye West: *Graduation*

50 Cent: *Curtis*

The same-day release (September 11, 2007) of these two albums caused some to see West's higher sales as a win for "conscious" rap over "gangsta" rap.

Taken from: *Billboard*, September 18, 2007. www.billboard.com/bbcom/news/article_display.jsp?vnu_content_id=1003642725.

It's called "raptivism," and some analysts believe it has the potential of the civil rights movement of the 1950s and '60s to transform America's political landscape.

"The potential is there, but it's still in its infant stage," says Carl Taylor of Michigan State University in East Lansing. "In one sense, they're much more powerful. [The earlier civil rights leaders] didn't have the avenue to parade the rage the rappers do."

The latent power of the movement became evident in June [2002] when almost 100,000 young people descended on New York's City Hall, joining teachers and labor activists to protest Mayor Michael Bloomberg's proposed $358 million cut in education funding. They came because rap entrepreneur Russell Simmons put out the call. But he also enticed them with a lineup of the industry's hottest hip-hop stars, such as Jay-Z and Chuck D.

Mr. Simmons, who founded Def Jam records, argues that hip-hop has always been the outlet for poor people's frustration, and if it parlays that energy into a political grass-roots movement, it can transform the nation. He founded the Hip-Hop Summit Action Network to fund community groups, arts programs, and political candidates. It's working with the Urban League on a literacy program and with the NAACP on a get-out-the-vote campaign.

But some of rap's elder statesmen, like Mr. Fisher, say the $5 billion industry needs to transform from within to become a more powerful and positive social force. Despite earlier efforts to stem the violence in some rap, heated verbal disputes between rappers have continued, sometimes resulting in killings—such as the still-unsolved deaths of Tupac Shakur and the Notorious B.I.G. several years ago.

Hip-Hop Peace Project Kicks Off

The National Hip-Hop Summit Youth Council, which grew out of Simmons' work, has been developing a "peace project" to address such issues. The group had planned on launching it in 2003. But last month's [October 2002] execution-style slaying of rap icon Jason Mizell, known as Jam Master Jay, prompted the artists and activists to dedicate their movement to him and roll out their agenda early.

"It took the death of a positive brother for all of us to wake up and say we have to put our foot forward now to make change," says Fisher, founder and chairman of the National Hip-Hop Summit Youth Council.

The project has several components: a code of principles designed to be used as a self-policing mechanism for the industry; an artist's mediation board to help resolve disputes between artists; a media complaint board; and a task force on gun, prison, and drug-law reform.

Chuck D, the frontman for Public Enemy, says the goal is not to censor or dictate artistic direction, but to ensure there's "balance." Too often, rap artists focus on the "gangsta fairy tale" without mentioning the repercussions, he says.

"I speak in jails, and everybody there says to me, 'Yo, what's going on with these rappers? They ain't never going to jail, talking about some fairy-tale gangsta life while we up here doing 10 to 15 years.

Members of Salt-N-Pepa participate in the Stop the Violence march in Brooklyn.

Nobody's telling our story,'" says Chuck D. "Kids needs to know the whole story."

But the proposed code is already generating controversy within the hip-hop community. Simmons, who's worked with Fisher over [the] years, has made it clear he believes any kind of code amounts to censorship and is opposed to it.

Rap Lyrics Reflect Reality

Some academics also caution against condemning rap's fury-filled lyrics without looking at the societal context from which they come. Murray Forman of Boston's Northeastern University argues that those lyrics give voice to violent, desperate experiences in the inner city that many in America don't want to admit exist.

"It's far too easy for the media to paint hip-hop as a problem," he says. "The other piece of it is that it's never been proven that representational violence leads to actual violence. There is desensitization, perhaps, and acceptance of a discourse of aggressiveness, but how that translates into actual aggressiveness is much more problematic."

Guy Ramsey of the University of Pennsylvania in Philadelphia also argues that rap is far more multifaceted than the media gives it credit for. "You can have a hip-hop artist like Mos Def who has a searing political critique, but it will never be talked about in the same way as some guy who's talking about whopping somebody," says Professor Ramsey.

Youth activist Kirkland doesn't disagree, but he argues that the growth of gangsta rap has had a clear impact on kids in the community.

"The hip-hop world and the gangsta world are about to collide, and we have to stop the body count," says Mr. Kirkland. "This is a life-and-death matter."

EVALUATING THE AUTHOR'S ARGUMENTS:

Marks argues that the hip-hop industry can serve as a platform for reducing the anger and violence that seem central to rap music. Do the activities cited have the potential to change the culture? What other methods could be used to encourage peace?

Viewpoint

3

Rap Music Lacks Political Impact and Is Largely Corporate Advertisements

Leonard Pitts Jr.

"It represents a corporatization of cool. . . ."

In the following viewpoint Leonard Pitts Jr. expresses his distaste for the way in which rap music has become so materialistic, invoking numerous brand names in its lyrics. Pitts laments the extent to which rappers spend so much effort on rapping about and endorsing and acquiring brand products, romanticizing the benefits of the consumption of certain material goods. Leonard Pitts Jr. is a news columnist for the *Miami Herald* and winner of the 2004 Pulitzer Prize for commentary. He is the author of *Becoming Dad: Black Men and the Journey to Fatherhood.*

AS YOU READ, CONSIDER THE FOLLOWING QUESTIONS:

1. According to the author, what was it that caused Jay-Z to boycott Cristal champagne?
2. What are some examples of product endorsements that Pitts claims show the materialism of rap?
3. Instead of free corporate advertising, what does Pitts believe rap should be?

I feel sorry for Shawn Carter. I know I shouldn't, but I do.

Jay-Z Angry at Cristal Makers

It seems that in recent weeks, Carter, a rap star and music executive known professionally as Jay-Z, has pronounced himself angry with the makers of Cristal champagne. Cristal, you should know, is frequently referenced in rap lyrics as a synonym for the high life, for pimping and drug dealing your way into an existence where the women are always willing, the luxury cars always gassed up, the sheets always satin.

This prompted the *Economist* magazine to ask Frederic Rouzaud, president of Champagne Louis Roederer, parent company of Cristal, whether it might hurt the brand's image to be associated with such a coarse, outlaw culture. Rouzaud's reply: "That's a good question, but what can we do? We can't forbid people from buying it. I'm sure Dom Perignon or Krug would be delighted to have their business."

Rap singers attend a Reebok promotional event highlighting recording artists and the sneakers custom-designed for them.

To which Jay-Z responded angrily. The rapper, who in his music has done as much as, or more than, anyone else to position Cristal as hip-hop's bubbly of choice, issued a statement decrying Rouzaud's "racist" statement and calling for a boycott.

Here it might be worthwhile to observe two facts.

One: Cristal has managed to thrive for most of 130 years without Jay-Z's endorsement. Indeed, the brand is manufactured sparingly and is perpetually sold out around the world.

Two: Cristal retails for upward of $200 a bottle. How, exactly, do you launch a boycott of something most people can't afford? Might as well ask me to boycott Gulfstream private jets while you're at it.

It is, on both sides, a silly contretemps. Still, there is something poignant in Jay-Z's apparent surprise and hurt at Cristal's blithe rejection of hip-hop's operating ethos: that acceptance can be bought.

Rap and Materialism

There has never been an entertainment form that placed as much faith in the healing virtues of materialism as rap. From the days when Run-DMC first extolled the virtues of Adidas shoes, rappers have invoked brand names and branded themselves with talismanic fervor. Timberland! Hennessy! Lexus! S. Carter!

They seem to feel that when you can afford these things, it makes you, I don't know . . . complete. As if, with Tims on your feet, Hennessy in your glass and a Lexus in your garage, you're good, you're covered, you're in the club.

For an art form whose artists and fans are largely young, largely black and largely from poor, bullet-scarred neighborhoods, it is a powerfully attractive fantasy. But it is a fantasy nevertheless. Which is, in so many words, what Frederic Rouzaud just brutally explained to Shawn Carter: that he is not in the club. That no matter how much Cristal he buys, he will never be in the club. Sure, kid, we'll take your money. But don't mistake that for respect. Not while you're young. And black. And reeking of nouveau riche. And representing values that are anathema to our own.

So yeah, I feel sorry for Carter. But at the same time, what's it tell you that he was even surprised?

Free Corporate Advertising

Among the many lies of hip-hop, this whole notion that wearing or imbibing or driving the proper brand will make you whole is in some ways the most infuriating. It represents a corporatization of cool that would have made Miles Davis ill. In his era, after all, cool meant being an iconoclast, a visionary threat to the status quo. In Jay-Z's era, it is a brand name, it has a sponsor, it can be bought off the rack.

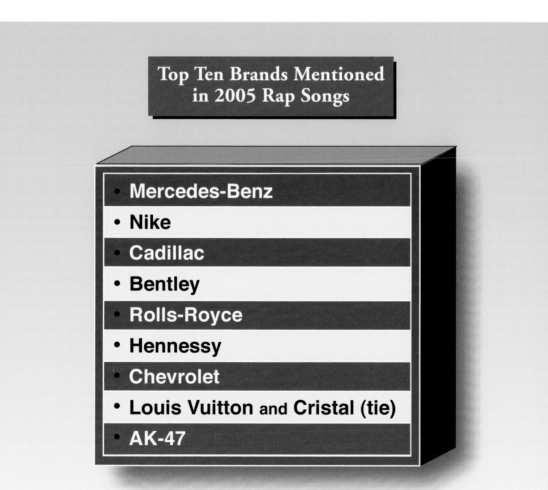

Top Ten Brands Mentioned in 2005 Rap Songs

- Mercedes-Benz
- Nike
- Cadillac
- Bentley
- Rolls-Royce
- Hennessy
- Chevrolet
- Louis Vuitton and Cristal (tie)
- AK-47

Taken from: "American Brandstand 2005" by Agenda, Inc.
http://money.cnn.com/2005/12/30/Autos/rap_brands/index.htm.

Rap could have been, should have been, a truth-teller and world-shaker. Instead it has largely contented itself with being free advertising for corporate titans, selling fake cool, sometimes with corporate assent, but often without even a thank-you. Brand names, it says, will make you whole. It is painful to know that Jay-Z has sold that lie to young people by the millions. What's more painful is that apparently, he also bought it himself.

EVALUATING THE AUTHOR'S ARGUMENTS:

In this viewpoint Pitts argues that rap has largely become a celebration of materialism. Do you agree with Pitts? Do other types of music focus on materialism?

Viewpoint 4

Rap Music Is a Powerful Political Tool

Ryan Smith and Swati Pandey

"The hip-hop nation has gone global, and it's going to change the world."

In the following viewpoint Ryan Smith and Swati Pandey argue that rap music and hip-hop culture are powerful political tools. They point to several examples that they say show this music form being used for political purposes. Smith and Pandey believe that music is a powerful political tool and that rap is no exception. Ryan Smith and Swati Padney are researchers for the *Los Angeles Times*.

AS YOU READ, CONSIDER THE FOLLOWING QUESTIONS:

1. What do the authors give as historical examples of songs used as political tools?
2. What do the authors give as contemporary examples of rap music and hip-hop culture used as political tools?
3. In what ways do Smith and Pandey argue that hip-hop is ideally suited for political impact?

Tomorrow's most powerful political voice won't be on CNN. Tune in to your iPod. In 1939, Billie Holiday crooned against the lynching of black men in her song "Strange Fruit." In 1969, Jimi Hendrix's version of "The Star-Spangled Banner" blasted peaceniks out of their drug dreams and into the streets.

Then, in 1989, came Public Enemy's "Fight the Power." That inchoate shout of rage against all forms of oppression is growing into a force of real potential. The hip-hop nation has gone global, and it's going to change the world.

It wasn't Al Sharpton, Jesse Jackson or Louis Farrakhan who cranked up debate about bigotry in the wake of Hurricane Katrina. It was rap star Kanye West's "Bush doesn't care about black people."

Music and Political Impact

Crispin Sartwell, a political science teacher at Dickinson College, Pennsylvania, says of the phenomenon: "If Thomas Paine or Karl Marx were [here] today, they might be issuing records rather than pamphlets."

West's words inspired the rapper David Banner and others to play a concert to support Hurricane Katrina victims. The Hip-Hop Caucus helped organise a march with black politicians to protest against police efforts to keep Katrina refugees out of the mostly white city of Gretna, Louisiana.

Hip-hop organisations such as the National Political Hip-Hop Convention started voter registration drives last year [2004], getting thousands of young people to vote for the first time. The Centre for Information and Research on Civic Learning and Engagement reported that in the 2004 presidential election "youth turnout increased substantially, and much of this increase was driven by an increase in voting among African American youth".

> **FAST FACT**
>
> Many universities now offer courses on hip-hop culture, which includes the study of rap music.

Music Travels Well

But hip-hop's greater potential comes from its technology-fuelled border-hopping power, with the internet and iPods carrying the

Rap Music and Politics

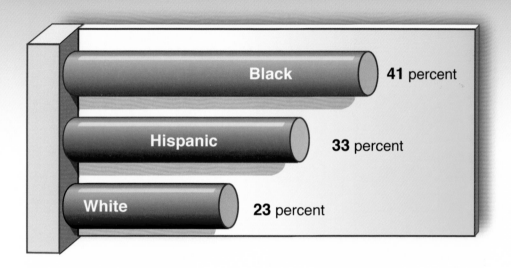

Percentage of youth who agree rap music videos should be more political:

Black — **41** percent

Hispanic — **33** percent

White — **23** percent

Taken from: Black Youth Project, June 2007.

beat to US military personnel in Baghdad and militant young Muslims alike. The genre is defining the war in Iraq the way psychedelic rock shaped memories of the Vietnam War, not only because it has become the music of protest but because it is the language of the soldiers, who make it themselves on simple equipment. Words over a beat.

Israelis rhyme about the intifada. In Britain, the Asian Dub Foundation sings about Tony Blair's entanglement in Iraq, while Ms Dynamite gives hip-hop a feminist touch.

Hip-hop travels like no other music. Any rapper can use a computer to layer a beat under a native melody and a rap about politics. This political potential revealed itself in the recent riots that shuddered through French suburbs.

Hip-Hop Is Ready

Can hip-hop overcome its occasional embrace of the thug life and "bling-bling" image and become a true political movement? Of

Peace activist Cindy Sheehan and rapper DMC, pictured, at a "Bring 'Em Home Now" benefit, show their support for withdrawal of troops from Iraq.

course. It is ready to take on failing schools, the effects of drugs, the despair of a low-wage economy, and warfare on city streets and foreign battlefields. The American dream is not credible. The calls for accountability are.

Kanye West stated a perception about Bush that was fed by the reality of the Administration's policies. Speaking truth to power, igniting passion and inspiring people to action—this is when music has always been most potent.

Hip-hop is a global party with a platform that is just beginning to take shape. What it already has is a mike and millions of ears.

EVALUATING THE AUTHORS' ARGUMENTS:

In this viewpoint Smith and Pandey argue that the rap music of hip-hop culture is becoming a powerful political tool. They claim that it can "overcome its occasional embrace of the thug life and the 'bling-bling' image and become a true political movement." Do you think the previous authors in this section would agree with them?

Rap Music Must Be Changed Through Dialogue and Cultural Change

Clarence Page

"To change rap, we must change the culture that feeds it."

In the following viewpoint Clarence Page reflects on what the civil rights activist, Martin Luther King Jr., would think about rap music culture. He argues that the majority of rap music conveys damaging messages about young black women. He argues that the solution to this is not censorship, but conversation about how to change the culture. Clarence Page is a columnist for the *Chicago Tribune,* where he writes a nationally syndicated column.

AS YOU READ, CONSIDER THE FOLLOWING QUESTIONS:

1. As cited by Page, what are some of the words in rap music used to describe young black women?
2. According to the author, what are some examples of the backlash against the portrayal of young black women in rap music?
3. What is the alternative to censorship, according to the author?

Clarence Page, "Cleaning Up Rap Music's Bad-Boy Culture Won't Be Easy," *Grand Rapids Press,* January 18, 2005, p. A7. Reproduced by permission.

M id-January is the time of year when countless orators turn into crystall ball gazers. In grand speeches across the land, they speculate as to what Martin Luther King Jr., who would have been 76 on [January 15, 2005], would think if he were still alive today.

Rap Music Culture

I wonder what he would think of today's rap music culture.

I wonder what he would think of a world in which young black poets refer to young black women as "ho's," "bitches," "chickenheads," "skeezers," "gold-diggers" and "hoochie mamas."

I wonder what he'd think of the 21st century minstrel show that hip-hop videos have given us with endless portrayals of black women as booty-shaking ornaments accessorizing the macho images of black males dressed-down in a ghetto-centric splendor appropriate for a prison yard.

Not all of rap is weak like that. As my 15-year-old son and personal hip-hop consultant is eager to inform me, today's rap world has swung largely away from the gangster rap of the 1980s and '90s toward the political and social "consciousness rap" of, say, Talib Kweli, Common or Kanye West, the producer-turned-rapper whose debut album *The College Dropout* with the religious hit "Jesus Walks" scored 10 Grammy nominations.

> **FAST FACT**
>
> According to a 2007 poll, half of those who listen to rap music and watch rap videos believe the media are at least a "somewhat accurate" representation of African American men and women.

A Growing Backlash

Despite such occasional glimmers of something resembling intelligence, the vast majority of rap video fare falls back on the same simplistic mother/whore stereotypes against which the mainstream women's movement has crusaded for decades. With that in mind, it is encouraging to see a new and remarkably broad-based backlash rising up to cast a critical light on hip-hop's narrow view of black women's sexuality.

Demonstrators across the country have attended rallies protesting the use of derogatory lyrics in rap music.

Essence, the highest-circulation black women's magazine, has launched a year-long examination of rap's treatment of women under the theme, "Take Back the Music." The project includes articles, a conference and a study of how music videos affect young viewers.

Essence editors say they decided to tackle rap images after protestors at the historically black women's Spelman College in Atlanta told the rap star Nelly not to come to a bone-marrow drive that his foundation was sponsoring on campus because his lyrics were too insulting to women. The event at a major black college marked an important departure from the silence with which most black students, fearful perhaps of being seen as uncool, have avoided much public criticism of rap stars.

The criticism from *Essence,* a major voice for upwardly mobile black women, is harder for the hip-hop industry and consumers to ignore than the complaints of Bill O'Reilly on Fox News Channel. When I checked its Web poll at www.essence.com last week, more than 72 percent of more than 2,700 respondents agreed that what they hear "about women in most songs played on urban stations makes me cringe."

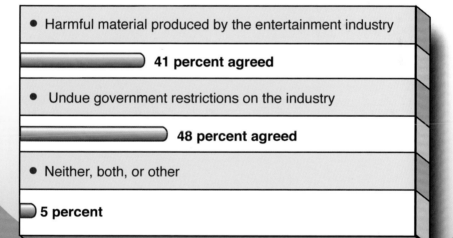

Violence, Sex, and Indecency: Government Restrictions and the Entertainment Industry

A survey asked Americans which is more harmful to society:

- Harmful material produced by the entertainment industry

41 percent agreed

- Undue government restrictions on the industry

48 percent agreed

- Neither, both, or other

5 percent

Americans have ambivalent views about the appropriate role for government in curbing sex, violence, and indecency in the entertainment media. They have doubts about the effectiveness of government action and believe that public pressure—in the form of complaints and boycotts—is a better way of dealing with the problem. They also blame audiences more than the media industry for objectionable material. Significantly, Americans see greater danger in the government's imposing undue restrictions on the entertainment industry than in the industry producing harmful content.

Taken from: Pew Research Center for the People & the Press survey conducted by Princeton Survey Research Associates International, March 17–21, 2005. http://people-press.org/reports/pdf/241.pdf.

Conversation, Not Censorship

But what is to be done? The project is "more about conversation than censorship," Michaela Angela Davis, *Essence* executive, fashion and beauty editor, said in an interview.

That's wise. Censorship is not the answer. It only makes the forbidden fruit more desirable, especially to the young and excitable. To change rap, we must change the culture that feeds it. And, to change attitudes, first we have to talk.

Nelly argues in the January [2005] *Essence* that "Women are in the (music) videos by choice. . . . Several women who have been in my videos have gone on to do TV appearances and movies. No one can dictate other people's choices and situations."

That's OK. Cultural change begins with conversations, freely expressed and from the heart. We African Americans too often silence ourselves with politically-correct "ghettocentric" notions that black-on-black criticism of any sort is a form of racial betrayal. Quite the opposite, it is our salvation. We betray each other if we fail to warn each other when we appear quite obviously to be destroying ourselves.

EVALUATING THE AUTHOR'S ARGUMENTS:

Page argues that rap music should not be censored. Do you agree? How could students at your school get involved in the conversation about rap culture?

Rap Music Must Be Changed by the Corporate Manufacturers

Glen Ford

"African Americans do not control the packaging and dissemination of their culture. . . ."

In the following viewpoint Glen Ford argues that the corporate manufacturers of rap, or hip-hop, music are to blame for the content. Ford claims that the independent, or socially conscious, rapper has no options for exposure, since this is not what the manufacturer wants to sell. Only the manufacturers, Ford claims, not the rappers or very young consumers, are to blame for the content of the music. Glen Ford was a founding member of the Washington chapter of the National Association of Black Journalists (NABJ) and is executive editor of the *Black Agenda Report.*

AS YOU READ, CONSIDER THE FOLLOWING QUESTIONS:

1. According to Ford, if McDonald's acted like rap music corporations, what would the social reaction be?
2. According to Ford, why can't "conscious" rappers reach the mass market?
3. Who is the target consumer of hip-hop, or rap, music, according to the author?

Glen Ford, "Hip Hop Profanity, Misogyny and Violence: Blame the Manufacturer," *Black Agenda Report,* May 2, 2007. Reproduced by permission.

O n a Spring day at McDonald's fast food restaurants all across Black America, counter clerks welcome female customers with the greeting, "What you want, bitch?" Female employees flip burgers in see-through outfits and make lewd sexual remarks to pre-teen boys while bussing tables. McDonald's managers position themselves near the exits, arms folded, Glocks protruding from their waistbands, nodding to departing customers, "Have a good day, motherf**kers. Y'all my niggas."

If Rap Music Were McDonald's

Naturally, the surrounding communities would be upset. A portion of their anger would be directed at the young men and women whose conduct was so destructive of the morals and image of African Americans. Preachers would rail against the willingness of Black youth to debase themselves in such a manner, and politicians would rush to introduce laws making it a crime for public accommodations employees to use profanity or engage in lewd or threatening behavior. However, there can be no doubt that the full wrath of the community and the state would descend like an angry god's vengeance on the real villain: the McDonald's Corporation, the purveyor of the fast food experience product.

Hip Hop music is also a product, produced by giant corporations for mass distribution to a carefully targeted and cultivated demographic market. Corporate executives map out multi-year campaigns to increase their share of the targeted market, hiring and firing subordinates—the men and women of Artists and Recordings (A&R) departments—whose job is to find the raw material for the product (artists), and shape it into the package upper management has decreed is most marketable (the artist's public persona, image, style and behavior). It is a corporate process at every stage of artist "development," one that was in place long before the artist was "discovered" or signed to the corporate label. What the public sees, hears and consumes is the end result of a process that is integral to the business model crafted by top corporate executives. The artist, the song, the presentation—all of it is a corporate product.

Yet, unlike the swift and certain public condemnation that would crash down upon our hypothetical McDonald's-from-Da Hood, the bulk of Black community anger at hip hop products is directed at foul-behaving artists, rather than the corporate Dr. Frankensteins that created and profit from them. As the great Franz Fanon would have understood perfectly, colonized and racially oppressed peoples internalize—take ownership—of the social pathologies fostered by the oppressor. Thus, the anti-social aspects of commercial hip hop

Some believe that music executives are responsible for promoting negative images in rap in order to sell more music.

are perceived as a "Black" problem, to be overcome through internal devices (preaching and other forms of collective self-flagellation), rather than viewed as an assault by hostile, outside forces secondarily abetted by opportunists within the group.

In order for our nightmare McDonald's analogy to more closely fit the music industry reality, all the fast food chains would have to provide the same type of profane, low-life, hyper-sexualized, life-devaluing service/product: "Bitch-Burgers" from Burger King, served with "Chronic-Flavored Fries," "Ho Wings" from KFC, dipped in too-hot "187 Murder Sauce." If you wanted fast food, you'd have to patronize one or the other of these thug-themed chains. So, too, with hip hop music.

What About Alternative Rap?

A handful of entertainment corporations exercise total control of the market, in incestuous (and illegal) conspiratorial concert with corporate-dominated radio. Successful so-called "independent" labels are most often mere subcontractors to the majors, dependent on them for record distribution and business survival. They are no more independent than the owner of a McDonald's franchise, whose product must conform to the standards set by global headquarters in Oak Brook, Illinois.

As "conscious" rapper Paris wrote in an article republished in BAR, April 25 [2007], there is no viable alternative to the corporate nexus for hip hop artists seeking to reach a mass audience. "WHAT underground?" said Paris. "Do you know how much good material is marginalized because it doesn't fit white corporate America's ideals of acceptability? Independents can't get radio or video play anymore, at least not through commercial outlets, and most listeners don't acknowledge material that they don't see or hear regularly on the radio or on T.V."

The major record labels actively suppress positive hip hop by withholding promotional support of both the above- and below-the-table variety. Hip hop journalist and activist Davey D reported that Erykah Badu and The Roots' Grammy-winning hit "You Got Me" was initially rejected by the corporate nexus due to its "overtly positive" message . . . "so palms were greased with the promise that key stations countrywide would get hot 'summer jam' concert acts in exchange for airplay. According to Questlove [of The Roots], more than $1 million in cash and resources were eventually laid out for the success of that single song."

Black America's hip hop problem cannot be laid at the feet of a few hundred wayward performers—and should certainly not be assigned to some inherent pathology in Black culture. African Americans do not control the packaging and dissemination of their culture: corporations and their Black comprador allies and annexes do. The mass Gangsta Rap phenomenon is a boardroom invention. I know.

What About the Consumers?

From 1987 to early 1994, I co-owned and hosted "Rap It Up," the first nationally syndicated radio hip hop music program. During the first half of this period, the Rap genre accomplished its national "breakout" from New York and LA, spreading to all points in between. By 1990, the major labels were preparing to swallow the independent labels that had birthed commercial hip hop, which had evolved into a wondrous mix of party, political and "street"-aggressive subsets. One of the corporate labels (I can't remember which) conducted a study that shocked the industry: The most "active" consumers of Hip Hop, they discovered, were "tweens," the demographic slice between the ages of 11 and 13.

The numbers were unprecedented. Even in the early years of Black radio, R&B music's most "active" consumers were at least two or three years older than "tweens." It didn't take a roomful of PhDs in human development science to grasp the ramifications of the data. Early and pre-adolescents of both genders are sexual-socially undeveloped—uncertain and afraid of the other gender. Tweens revel in honing their newfound skills in profanity; they love to curse. Males, especially, act out their anxieties about females through aggression and derision. This is the cohort for which the major labels would package their hip hop products. Commercial Gangsta Rap was born—a sub-genre that

Rap and Responsibility

In 2007, 345 people responded to an online poll by the hip-hop site SOHH.com, which asked:

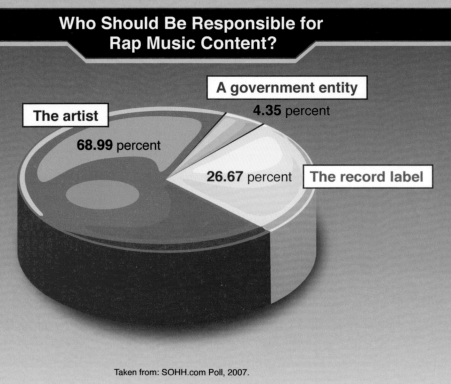

Who Should Be Responsible for Rap Music Content?

A government entity
4.35 percent

The artist
68.99 percent

26.67 percent | **The record label**

Taken from: SOHH.com Poll, 2007.

would lock a whole generation in perpetual arrested social development.

First, the artists would have to be brought into the corporate program. The term "street" became a euphemism for a monsoon of profanity, gratuitous violence, female and male hyper-promiscuity, the most vulgar materialism, and the total suppression of social consciousness. A slew of child acts was recruited to appeal more directly to the core demographic.

Women rappers were coerced to conform to the new order. A young female artist broke down at my kitchen table one afternoon, after we had finished a promotional interview. "They're trying to make me into a whore," she said, sobbing. "They say I'm not 'street' enough."

Her skills on the mic were fine. "They" were the A&R people from her corporate label.

Stories like this abounded during the transition from independent to major label control of hip hop. The thug- and -"ho"ification of the genre is now all but complete.

Blame the manufacturer.

EVALUATING THE AUTHORS' ARGUMENTS:

In this viewpoint Glen Ford claims that the corporate manufacturer of rap music is to blame for the content. What do you think Clarence Page, author of the previous viewpoint, would say to Ford? What would Ford say to Page?

Chapter 2

Is Rap Music Harmful to Women?

Rap music is frequently charged with depicting women as objects or props.

Rap Music Is Damaging to Black Women

Johnnetta B. Cole and Beverly Guy-Sheftall

"The power of words— and the attitudes they reflect— cannot be ignored."

In the following viewpoint Johnnetta B. Cole and Beverly Guy-Sheftall argue that the negative references to women in rap music do have a damaging effect on women. Because rap music has a particularly strong influence on black youth, and also due to the history of social hatred of black women, they claim that the damaging effects are primarily on young black women.

Johnnetta B. Cole is the president of Bennett College for Women and the president emerita of Spelman College, the two historically black colleges for women in the United States. Beverly Guy-Sheftall is the founding director of the Women's Research and Resource Center and the Anna Julia Cooper Professor of Women's Studies at Spelman College.

AS YOU READ, CONSIDER THE FOLLOWING QUESTIONS:

1. According to the authors, how do gangsta and booty rap define what it is to be a man?

2. What are some of the lyrics in rap music that the authors find misogynistic and disrespectful toward black girls and women?
3. Who do the authors think is responsibile for changing the language and images of rap music?

There has been a major war brewing (simmering, erupting—back to simmering again) between Black men and women since the sixties, and hip-hop is a significant and influential site of contemporary gender battles. According to hip-hop critic-historian Nelson George, this cultural war between the sexes has been fought with words, books, magazines, movies, and rap music. . . .

Alienation Between the Sexes

A critical discussion of the gender politics of the music that in profound ways defines the hip-hop generation certainly opens up the possibility of a long-overdue cross-generational dialogue between our women and men, our youth and elders. In his book *The Hip Hop Generation* (2002), cultural critic Bakari Kitwana defines the demographic segment with which we are concerned [here] as African Americans born between 1965 and 1984, and he uses the term *hip-hop generation* interchangeably with *Black youth culture*. Contrasting the different worlds of "them" and "us," he asserts:

> For our parents' generation, the political ideals of civil rights and Black power are central to their worldview. Our parents' generation placed family, spirituality, social responsibility, and Black pride at the center of their identity as Black Americans. They, like their parents before them looked to their elders for values and identity. The core set of values shared by a large segment of the hip-hop generation . . . stands in contrast to our parents' worldview. For the most part, we have turned to ourselves, our peers, global images and products, and the new realities we face for guidance. . . . Central to our identity is a severe sense of alienation between the sexes.

This severe sense of alienation between the sexes is most notably reflected in the frequent descriptions of Black girls and women as "bitches," "hos," "skeezers" "freaks," "gold diggers," "chickenheads," and "pigeons." Rap music videos are notorious for featuring half-clothed young Black women gyrating obscenely and functioning as backdrops, props, and objects of lust for rap artists who sometimes behave as predators. While gangsta rap, which emerged in the late eighties, is often described as a contemporary expression of youthful political radicalism, it seems as though the resentment, hostility, and disdain that many young Black men feel toward the police and "the System" have been directed at Black females. It appears that too many of our young men are blaming young women and treating them as part of the problem, rather than as cherished lovers and potential life partners. Kitwana suggests that the continuing popularity of rappers' women-hating lyrics and the gender conflicts they disclose are a disturbing reflection of the tension brewing between young Black women and men. He is not suggesting, however, that this "gender divide" began with the hip-hop generation: "The persistence of old attitudes about gender roles, rooted deep in American and Black cultures and strongly shaped by popular culture and Judeo-Christian ethics, has helped to breed cynicism between young Black men and women."

Rap Music Leads to Disrespect

We are aware that rap music is where many young Blacks get their problematic gender messages and [as Kitwana contends] that "due to its role in shaping a whole generation's worldview, including [their] ideas about sex, love, friendship, dating, and marriage, rap music is critical to any understanding of the hip-hop generation's gender crisis." We are concerned because we believe that hip-hop is more misogynist and disrespectful of Black girls and women than other popular music genres. The casual references to rape and other forms of violence and the soft-porn visuals and messages of many rap music videos are seared into the consciousness of young Black boys and girls at an early age. The lyrics, images—and attitudes that undergird them—are potentially harmful to Black girls and women in a culture that is already negative about our humanity, our sexuality, and our overall worth. They are also harmful to Black boys and men because they encourage misogynistic attitudes and behaviors.

We are also aware that contentious debates will continue about whether in fact certain forms of rap music, which Los Angeles–based gangsta rapper, actor, and former gang member Ice T calls simply "the art of shit talking," are harmful. He defends the music by indicating that it is harmless boasting on the part of ghetto men with few outlets for expression, and has very little connection to reality. He also says he learned early on that telling a nasty story, especially about sex, would get him more listeners than rhyming and rapping about politics. . . . He also says that his rap is reality-based, and that what he says is "real" because it is a reflection of how he lives and talks, and how disempowered men in his neighborhood live and talk. Whether what rappers sing about is "real" or fantasy, we do not believe, as Ice T argues, that it has no meaning. . . .

At the very least we are convinced that his unacknowledged class biases with respect to women have consequences in the "real" world and are manifest in the attitudes of many young women and men who believe it's all right to treat *certain* women disrespectfully and label them "bitches" and "hos" because that's who they are and that's what they deserve. In other words, classism and sexism are the twin burdens of poor black women. . . .

Some Rap Lyrics Make Black Women the "Enemy"

At the core of the gender politics of hip-hop is a pervasive and profound ambivalence toward Black women and the portrayal of relations between the sexes as primarily conflictual. In an important study of gangsta rap's influence on college students' actual attitudes, and potentially their behavior, Professor Bruce Wade and his student Cynthia Thomas-Gunnar present a compelling argument that "explicit [rap] lyrics are generally inappropriate and harmful to society." They discovered that contemporary Black college students, especially men, believe that rap music accurately portrays gender relations. Is it any wonder then, since the music frequently communicates a general hostility, distrust, and disregard for Black women as anything other than atomized body parts and sex objects, that the study concluded that men who listen to rap music favorably were more likely to harbor attitudes that could be described as rape-prone?

Given the enormous popularity of hip-hop and gangsta rap, this is certainly a frightening and explosive finding. It confirms many critics' beliefs that rap music has an undeniable and adverse influence on its young listeners. Certain rap music lyrics, particularly gangsta rap, are apparently effective at communicating a dangerous message: that the enemy of Black urban youth is not just the police or poverty, not only an unjust system, but Black women and girls as well. Songs like "Trust No Bitch, Trust No Hoe" and "Bitch Betta Have My Money" portray Black women as predatory, untrustworthy, and worthless.

In many of these music videos, women are stripped of any humanizing subjective identity, since the viewer observes only body parts, and the script is usually what social critic Michael Eric Dyson refers to as the rappers' "subterranean, pornographic fantasies." Often described as "booty

Some people feel that young women are negatively influenced by the images of scantily clad women appearing in rap videos.

rap," this form of rap is "characterized by an obsession with sex and perverted eroticism, visually backed by scantily clothed women mimicking sex and sometimes actually performing it on stage," according to [hip-hop critic William Eric] Perkins. As evidenced by the lyrics of Underground Kingz (UGK), even pedophilia becomes fair game in this distorted and unreal world of rap, sex, and violence. In an *Essence* article that asks "Are Music Videos Pimping Our Girls?" self-described hip-hop feminist Joan Morgan believes "it's up to us to identify these videos for what they are—adult content that shouldn't be shown in prime time."

Artistic Expression or Real Hate?

What is the danger of gangsta rap's *femiphobia* [fear and disdain of the female], borrowing Dyson's terminology? What happens when a young man's perceptions of women have been shaped by the misogynistic messages he's heard for most of his life and what he has seen on countless music videos? To be sure, women are likely to be robbed of their humanity and viewed both artistically and perhaps in real life mainly as objects of male sexual fantasies. The line between hyperbolic lyrics and real hate language has become increasingly blurred in gangsta rap. Moreover, the celebrated "thug life" does not just provide a creative source for rap lyrics, it actually intrudes upon the lives of rappers like Tupac Shakur and Notorious B.I.G. as their jail sentences, drug charges, gun shoot-outs, and ultimately their deaths reveal. . . .

Popular Culture Treats Women as Objects

While examining the values that many young men and women are encouraged to embrace, we are mindful of the fact that they have come of age in a time when women—especially young, sexually desirable women—are viewed by a sex-obsessed dominant culture as sex objects rather than as multidimensional beings deserving of love and respect. When males and the male-controlled media treat young women as objects, they often see themselves in the same manner. This insidious dynamic is certainly not entirely new, but with so much of popular culture representing young women as half-naked, promiscuous, man-hungry, and lacking in self-esteem, internalized sexism is one likely result. Poet and social critic Sonia Sanchez describes this phenomenon as the country trying to "asphyxiate our daughters in a state of undress, and convince them that they're hos. Even in college they [try to make them] hos. Any place [young women] walk, the country says, 'I'm going to take you back to hoedom.'"

Similarly, young people are ensconced in a mass culture of crass materialism that places financial gain and the mindless consumption of material goods over healthy, productive, loving relationships. Some rappers have made millions rapping about women giving up sex in exchange for liquor, jewelry, and less. The message that young Black women's bodies can be purchased cheaply on the open market is a grim, modern-day reminder of slavery. In some ways, Black women are still on the auction block! What makes this scenario so devastating, however, is that it is our own men, the young ones to whom our future will soon be entrusted, who are frequently doing the bidding and buying in this century. And much too often our young women are selling themselves, metaphorically speaking, in a desperate and misguided search for love and "security." . . .

The Power of Words

To be sure, the ultimate responsibility for shifting the language and images now pervasive in some strands of rap music lies within Black communities. Several African American leaders are committed to continuing meeting with leading hip-hop producers and superstar performers with hopes of persuading them to use the power of their lyrics to communicate more positive, empowering messages. The most prominent leader to wage war on rap music while also calling for dialogue with rap artists has been the Reverend Calvin Butts, pastor of Harlem's famous Abyssinian Baptist Church. An outspoken organizer at the 1993 protest rally in New York City during which he called for censorship, the Reverend Butts continues his advocacy efforts for major reforms in the rap community despite their First Amendment rights to free speech. More of us, on an individual and collective level, must challenge degrading images of women, boycott music that perpetuates hate and gratuitous violence, and talk, talk, talk with one another in our schools, universities, churches, mosques, and community centers about how we can move a more solution-oriented gender debate into the public arena. We must continue to dialogue with artists and producers of rap about creating more affirming, socially conscious messages. We must demand that songs with countermessages get more air time, such as BWP's "NO means NO!" and A Tribe Called Quest's "Date Rape," which assails acquaintance violence. We must address ways of countering the low self-esteem that plagues many of our young people to the point where they demean themselves with words and images as powerful as shackles, whips, and nooses. . . .

In the October 2002 issue of *Ebony*, editor Lerone Bennett Jr.'s hard-hitting article, "Sex and Music: Has It Gone Too Far?" labels this sexually explicit music "macho-macho," and articulates the ways in which it is harmful to Black communities. He is also clear about what we must do: "We also need a new understanding—in the media, in the entertainment industry, in our churches, schools and organizations—that popular songs are as important as civil rights bills and that a society that pays pipers to corrupt its young and to defame its women and mothers will soon discover that it has no civil rights to defend and no songs to sing."

The power of words—and the attitudes they reflect—cannot be ignored. The hateful and harsh gender talk in too much of rap music and American popular culture must be addressed by socially conscious women and men who deplore violence and misogyny, and understand the damage it does within our communities and around the world.

EVALUATING THE AUTHORS' ARGUMENTS:

In this viewpoint, the authors argue that the lyrics of rap music and the images of rap music videos have negative effects. Some might argue that rap music is "only music" or, like rapper Ice T says, it doesn't mean anything. What do you think?

Negative Images of Black Women Do Not Stem from Rap

"This music is a reaction to emotions of anger, frustration and inequity of mostly young minority people. . . ."

Nida Khan

In the following viewpoint, Nida Khan rejects the idea that the rap music of hip-hop culture should be blamed for the damaging treatment of women in our culture. Instead of looking to the music, Khan argues that we need to recognize that the music reflects the misogyny of our culture. She believes that we should take the focus off of the music and look at the broader culture and media representation.

Nida Khan is a hip-hop journalist who has written articles for the *Source Magazine*, Vibe.com, *XXL Magazine*, and *MTV News Online*, among others.

AS YOU READ, CONSIDER THE FOLLOWING QUESTIONS:

1. According to the author, what sorts of societal ills does rap music mirror?
2. Instead of blaming rap music, where does the author think we should look for the causes of misogyny?
3. Why does the author believe that media companies will not promote positive messages?

Nida Khan, "In Defense of Hip-Hop," *Women's Media Center*, May 18, 2007. Reproduced by permission.

"Hip-hop is the CNN of the ghetto"—words spoken by legendary artist Chuck D of Public Enemy years before Puffy became a household name and bling a term used by actual CNN anchors. Serving as a mirror to such societal ills as poverty, injustice, drugs and violence, hip-hop—or more specifically rap music—has brought realities of urban life and mainstream systematic privilege to the forefront of discussion. MCs, aka rappers, have opened wounds that many would prefer remained covered via methods that both educate and entertain. Now this mechanism for empowerment and communication is under attack yet again.

Scapegoating Hip-Hop

While Don Imus searched for a defense against his use of the now notorious words "nappy headed hos" in reference to the Rutgers women's basketball team, he was successful in scapegoating the often-targeted genre of hip-hop. But what Imus and the average citizen fail to grasp is the foundation of this culture or the notion that what you hear on radio airwaves and see on TV doesn't encompass the plethora of diversity within the music.

For several years I've worked within the hip-hop industry in a multitude of capacities. From my vantage point at record labels, recording studios and finally as a music journalist, I've had the honor of sitting down and picking the brains of many hip-hop poets. And *poetry* and *expression* is exactly what they produce: words and ideas conjured over the hottest beats. Rappers take complex ideas and transform them into catchy lyrics and rhyming sequences with astuteness and intense precision. Imagine the endless boundaries of MCs if they were all given equal access to education and opportunity that we espouse but rarely see in this country. A chance to pursue the American Dream is precisely what rappers under attack have worked to achieve. Take a look at the 50 Cents and Jay-Zs of the world. Self-made millionaires,

> **FAST FACT**
>
> Among rap artists with album sales over 20 million are at least four female artists: Lauryn Hill, Missy Elliott, Lil' Kim, and Foxy Brown.

they battled extreme circumstances and in the process established companies that employ and empower others shut out of corporate America.

In response to the ongoing controversy, several people have stepped forward. "We are proactive, not just reactive to the Don Imus so-called backlash," explains Dr. Ben Chavis, president/CEO of Russell Simmons's Hip-Hop Summit Action Network, after he and Simmons made recommendations for the recording industry to bleep the words ho, bitch and nigger on the airwaves and on clean CDs. "The truth is misogyny is not a hip-hop created problem. Misogyny is a deep-seated American society problem that is embedded in the historical evolution of the United States as a nation." The recommendations are meant, he says, to forestall governmental intrusion "on the rights of artists in a democratic society. This is important, and there are some in the media

The Gender Pay Gap, 1960–2003

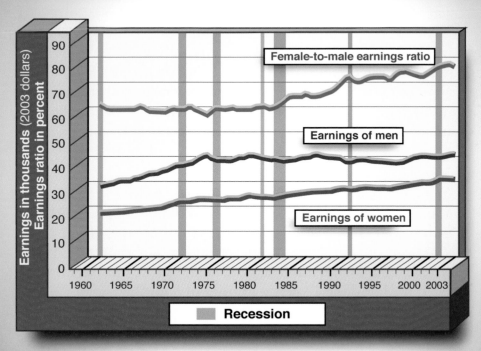

Female-to-Male Earnings Ratio and Median Earnings of Full-Time, Year-Round Workers 15 Years Old and over by Sex: 1960 to 2003

Taken from: U.S. Census Bureau, Current Population Survey, 1961 to 2004 Annual Social and Economic Supplements.

that just don't get it. Self regulation by the industry is not censorship. Good corporate social responsibility is not censorship."

Media Representation at Large Is to Blame

The shift in dynamic from Imus to hip-hop utterly amazes me. Granted I don't condone use of words like ho and bitch towards myself or any other woman, but I understand along with Dr. Ben that rap music isn't the only forum where we see this. Why don't we target the representation of women and people of color in Hollywood? Why don't we go after the millionaire and billionaire movie directors/producers of the world who represent minority women a majority of the time as the exotic other or the overly sexualized temptress, and minority men as criminals? Before blaming everything on one facet, we need to analyze all of pop culture and media representation at large.

MCs may have an audience via their music, but until you see a Snoop Dogg or a Ludacris with his own televised programming in mainstream news you simply can't juxtapose Imus and hip-hop. Until rappers have the kind of major network platform that Imus had and will have again, they are not fair game for attack. On the contrary, we need to explore and criticize why we see so few people of color on these networks or working behind-the-scenes in newsrooms in the first place. For those that are quick to jump on the criticism bandwagon, do they first understand that rap music's foundation was a check on society? That it was a mechanism for the powerless to speak their mind? Do they understand a history of socially and politically conscious music that was designed to mobilize people? Even today, this music is a reaction to emotions of anger, frustration and inequity of mostly young minority people surviving in a society where the pendulum of justice swings away from them most of the time.

The Futility of Targeting Record Labels

In attempts to curb some of the criticism against this form of expression, moves by Dr. Ben Chavis, Russell Simmons and even Rev. Al Sharpton were aimed at targeting the true culprits behind negative/misogynistic music—record labels and corporations. On May 3 [2007], Tamika Mallory of Sharpton's National Action Network led a March for Hip-Hop Decency in front of Sony, Universal Records and the Time Warner building in Manhattan.

Rap artist and actor Ice-T hopes a new hip-hop exhibit at the Smithsonian draws more mainstream attention to black culture and history.

"We cannot allow people to use the concept of freedom of speech and censorship as a shield for those who seek to denigrate any members of our society," she explains. "Freedom of speech is critical to freedom but so is the responsibility that comes with it. We are not saying that rappers or anyone cannot speak in any manner they choose. We are saying that record and media companies shouldn't support it if it crosses the line of sexism, racism and homophobia."

Sounds like a wonderful idealistic thought without a doubt, except for the fact that these companies and media outlets have profited countless billions off the backs of rappers, hip-hop culture and the community. It's incredibly difficult for artist/groups with positive or socially conscious messages like a Dead Prez to get signed, and if they do, never will they see radio spins or record sales like their negative counterparts. In an industry where marketing and radio promotion departments ensure that only certain albums get proper financial backing to guarantee air play and press, many talented people simply get shelved. Radio stations themselves have specific daily play lists, in effect brainwashing the masses with the same songs and the same messages. I've had rappers straight out tell me that they wanted to go with a specific single from their album but were forced to go with something else. And others have simply said they put out a single about women and money to reel in listeners to a deeper, profound meaning on the album that might otherwise have been ignored. Interesting isn't it?

Don't Blame Hip-Hop

These days Don Imus is at his ranch contemplating his next move. Chances are he'll return to the airwaves in some capacity in little time, while the young woman or man using music as a means to escape the all but insurmountable obstacles set in her/his path will find it ever more difficult because the world is now watching with keen eyes. For those who are new to this genre of poetic expression, I suggest watching the new Bruce Willis/Queen Latifah documentary, "Hip-Hop Project." It beautifully captures the essence of what this culture was, is and should be about. Until critics begin to fully comprehend the many layers of hip-hop, its historical context and place in society, they should listen to what the Godfather of it all said to me the other day—the man who literally started hip-hop with two turntables—DJ Kool Herc: "Tell all the geniuses to back off of hip-hop. Leave hip-hop alone."

EVALUATING THE AUTHORS' ARGUMENTS:

In this viewpoint the author defends rap music from the charge that it is responsible for the damaging treatment of women. Unlike Cole in the previous article, Khan believes that the music does not create the situation for women but merely reflects a situation that already exists. Do you agree that rap music merely reflects what is already a reality?

Viewpoint

3

Black Women Should Work to Stop the Damaging Images of Rap Music

Beverly Daniel Tatum

"These images could not exist without black participation."

In the following viewpoint Beverly Daniel Tatum argues that the portrayal of black women in hip-hop, or rap, music and videos is damaging to black women. She claims that what is particularly disturbing about this portrayal is the fact that black men and women are participants in the perpetuation of these images. She concludes that it will take more than the actions of black women to stop them. Beverly Daniel Tatum is the president of Spelman College and the author of *Why Are All the Black Kids Sitting Together in the Cafeteria? And Other Conversations About Race.*

1. According to Tatum, what is the global consequence for black women of the degrading images in rap music and videos?
2. Historically, who were the creators of negative black stereotypes, according to the author?
3. According to Tatum, why cannot black women alone change rap music and videos?

This year [2005], the editors of *Essence* magazine and more than 1,000 Spelman College students gathered to talk with representatives from the entertainment industry and cultural critics about the negative portrayals of black women in hip-hop music and videos.

Inspired by the May 2004 protest launched at Spelman in response to rap artist Nelly's "Tip Drill" video, the meeting was part of the *Essence* Take Back the Music campaign designed to further the Spelman dialogue and promote positive action to bring about change in how black women are depicted.

Just a Video?

The hypersexualized representations of black women as objects of degradation and violence found in both the lyrics and video images are exported globally to eager hip-hop fans around the world.

So what's the big deal, some might ask. It's only a video. But these videos help define the reality of young women who find themselves at risk of being treated on the streets like the women in the videos. While an affront in the United States, such treatment is especially painful when studying abroad, encountering global neighbors whose only previous encounter with black women has been through videos shown on cable networks.

Spelman students asked important questions about social responsibility on the part of the media and the artists. The most powerful question came from a sophomore who described herself as having grown up with hip-hop music. "What I want to know," she said, "is what did we do?" Why, she wanted to know, was she being repeatedly called a "bitch" or a "ho" and portrayed on screen as though she had no self-respect?

It was a question without an answer.

The History of Stereotypes

There is a long history of stereotypical images in the media of black people, portrayed as unintelligent, lazy and oversexed, dating back to before the Civil War. However, the original creators of these stereotypes were white people, often performing in blackface. Later, when black actors were employed in media roles, the creators still were most often white men. In contemporary hip-hop, while white financiers still play a role, the creators of many of the most offensive images are black people.

African-Americans have always had to struggle against internalizing the negative messages about who we are. "Black is beautiful" is a message that requires positive reinforcement in a culture that glorifies European images of beauty and has been historically reluctant to acknowledge the intellectual contributions of people of African descent.

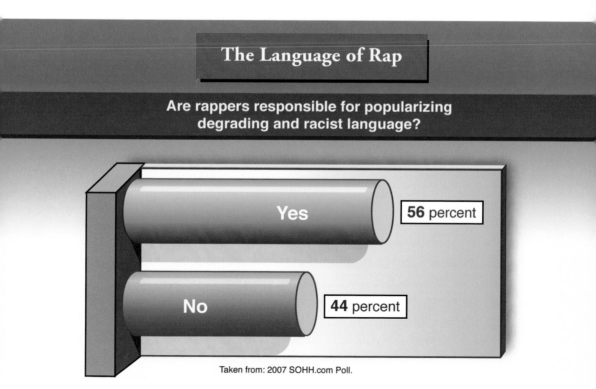

The Language of Rap

Are rappers responsible for popularizing degrading and racist language?

Yes — 56 percent

No — 44 percent

Taken from: 2007 SOHH.com Poll.

The My Black Is Beautiful movement encourages black women to define and promote their own beauty standards instead of being subject to stereotypes.

Both black men and women have been the victims of stereotyping. But the current derogatory depictions of black women by black men and the violence and disrespect that often accompanies these images can only be detrimental to the young people who view them. They perpetuate racist images in the minds of white viewers but also diminish self-respect and aspirations of young black men and women who view them.

Who Creates the Images?

For young black women, the fact that these images are presented by the same men who could be their fathers, brothers or husbands is especially disturbing, as is the participation of the young black women who are paid to be in the videos. These images could not exist without black participation.

Columnist Stanley Crouch has hailed the activism of Spelman students in response to these images as the birth of an important social movement—perhaps the most significant movement of their generation.

It is a movement in which they will need allies. Even if all black women stopped listening and purchasing music that degrades them, there are more than enough other consumers to keep the images alive. What did we do? It is a question without an answer, but one that calls for our attention.

> **EVALUATING THE AUTHOR'S ARGUMENTS:**
>
> In this viewpoint Tatum claims that while black women play a role in creating the images, they will need allies to stop the degradation. Do you agree? Who do you think is responsible for the content in rap music?

Black Women Should Create Their Own Images in Rap Music

Yvonne Bynoe

"Black women in hip-hop have to fight for power. . . ."

In the following viewpoint Yvonne Bynoe argues that the underlying problem with the message about black women in rap or hip-hop music is that it is the only message being heard. Bynoe believes that if black women had more power throughout the media, including within rap or hip-hop, there would be enough diversity in the portrayal of black women to render degrading messages in certain rap songs of small consequence. Yvonne Bynoe is the author of *Stand and Deliver: Political Activism, Leadership and Hip Hop Culture* and *The Encyclopedia of Rap and Hip Hop Culture.*

AS YOU READ, CONSIDER THE FOLLOWING QUESTIONS:
1. What is the author's primary objection to the portrayal of women in rap, or hip-hop, music?
2. According to Bynoe, why do black women need to address sexism in addition to racism against black women?
3. What are some examples of the actions that Bynoe suggests black women can take to fight for power?

Yvonne Bynoe, "Hip-Hop's (Still) Invisible Women," AlterNet.org, May 16, 2007. Reproduced by permission.

Ten years ago, journalists along with average joes and janes were discussing whether or not "hip-hop hates women," and regrettably today many within hip-hop are still debating that same question. In a 1995 essay, *Vibe* magazine's current editor-in-chief, Danyel Smith, discussed how hip-hop tended to mirror the biases of the greater society saying, "Women's versions of reality are somehow suspect; men's interpretations of women and their motives and ideas are considered more real than women's declarations."

The title of her article "Ain't a Damn Thing Changed," about sums up contemporary women's status within hip-hop. In the intervening years hip-hop generation women have not become visible, insofar that they have not staked out spaces that allow their stories and complex realities to be heard by the masses. Whether it is fear or access to capital or some combination of the two, hip-hop generation women have not created our version of the Lilith Fair to support female rap artists. Similarly, most female rap artists, like their male counterparts have not created independent record companies and touring apparatus that would allow them to control their messages and images, get those messages to the public and make money in the process. Subsequently, male rap artists (aided by their corporate entertainment entities), rather than black women themselves, have largely shaped the image of black women in the United States and in doing so have defined the contours of our public dialogue about black women.

> **FAST FACT**
>
> Since Nielsen SoundScan began tracking sales in 1991, only 13 female rappers have appeared on the year-end chart out of a pool of 585 artists.

Diversity of Portrayals Needed

For years many black women have had a tortured relationship with hip-hop: loving its beats, its energy, but hating the misogyny and gratuitous violence. The thing that appears to have changed is that more young black women, rather than critically examining their allegiance to the hip-hop status quo are now helping to maintain it. Several years ago, when women at Spelman College in Atlanta threatened to protest

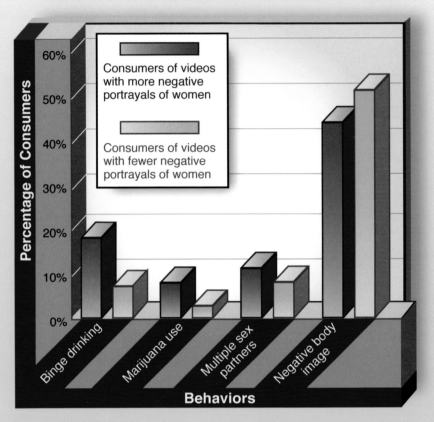

Rap Video Consumption and Behaviors of African American Adolescent Girls

Consumers of videos with more negative portrayals of women

Consumers of videos with fewer negative portrayals of women

Percentage of Consumers

60%
50%
40%
30%
20%
10%
0%

Binge drinking Marijuana use Multiple sex partners Negative body image

Behaviors

Taken from: Shani H. Peterson, Gina M. Windgood, Ralph J. DiClemente, Kathy Harrington, and Susan Davies, *Journal of Women's Health* 16(8), 2007. www.liebertonline.com/doi/pdfplus/10.1089/jwh.2007.0429.

Nelly's appearance on campus because of his music video "Tip Drill," young black women joined young black men in attacking the black female activists. Young black women parroted the lines that in the past were used by black men to rationalize misogyny in rap music such as "Hos do exist," "It's just entertainment" and "No one is forcing these women to be in these videos."

While all of these statements may indeed be true, they miss the point. At core the argument is not about whether every rap song has to be deep or whether women have the right to shake their money-makers in a music video; it is about whether black women gyrating on poles for dollars should be the sole portrayal of black women in our society. In echoing the words of activist and author Barbara Smith, women's studies has flourished in academia and has opened the doors for talented scholars such as Gwendolyn Pough and Tracy Sharpley-Whiting to publish groundbreaking books on women in hip-hop, but it has been less successful in educating, nurturing and raising the consciousness of young black women, in and out of the 'hood.

In our communities, we still refer to black men as "endangered species." We are rightfully alarmed about the staggering number of black men who are incarcerated each year and by the high number of young black men who drop out of school, leaving themselves unqualified for the legal job market. Unfortunately, there is far less urgency about the increasing incidences of HIV/AIDs among black women or the rise in young women of color going to jail or the plight of working, single mothers who cannot find safe, reliable and affordable childcare.

Focusing on Sexism Does Not Negate Racism

Asserting that young black women have needs and concerns that are particular to their gender, class and race in no way negates the important issues that are pertinent to young black men. Moreover, mature, really progressive politics understands that the fight for equality does not exclude women. Young black men and women seem to be making the same mistake that some of our elders did by pitting the ravages of racism against the tyranny of sexism and concluding that racism is more evil. As has been said by far more articulate people, even if racism ended tomorrow, gender discrimination would still exist.

As black women and black men, our ultimate strength will lie in our ability and our desire to jointly bring our distinct experiences, grievances and issues to the table and work in coalition toward manifesting an equitable and free society. What hip-hop generation women have to realize is that standing by passively, in the name of comradeship, afraid to anger the brothers has garnered us neither respect nor equality (assuming that the two can be separated). As was the case in prior generations, young black women need to step into the arena and forcefully speak their truths because: The black men who really don't like us will always find solace in the arms of others and use our strength as their excuse; the black men who merely like us will demand that we "play our position" so that they can gain power; and the black men who genuinely love us will fight alongside us for justice and will encourage us to fully express our hearts, minds and spirits.

Women Need to Take Action

The most political first step that many women within hip-hop can make is to create communities that nurture us: spaces where we can perform our own rhymes, spaces where we can share our own stories and spaces where we can give each other love and provide support. Author and activist Rebecca Walker made a profound statement when she said that our life's journey is about understanding our own suffering and how the powerful societal stratifications of race, class, gender and sexuality impact us all negatively. Women therefore cannot change sexism within hip-hop or in the broader society until we are willing to heal ourselves. When it is all said and done, railing against [controversial radio and television host Don] Imus or lobbying entertainment executives will not end sexism any more than Robitussin will cure cancer.

Queen Latifah, right, presents a $10,000 grant to Yvonne Pointer for founding "Postive Plus," an organization focusing on helping women seize control of their destiny.

Black women in hip-hop have to fight for power—be willing to love and respect ourselves enough to put the financial, intellectual and creative energy behind establishing our own blogs, websites, podcasts, e-newsletters, record companies, music conferences, summits, publishing companies, magazines, radio shows and television programs that illuminate the many sides of beautiful black womanhood. We also have to be brave enough to collaborate with each other, with women of other races and with equality-seeking men to make these new entities the mainstream rather than the alternative.

EVALUATING THE AUTHORS' ARGUMENTS:

In this viewpoint Bynoe emphasizes the need for black women to get the power to represent themselves in the media, while the previous viewpoint by Tatum emphasizes the need to seek to end negative representations of black women in rap music. Which strategy do you think would be more successful in altering people's views about black women?

Does Rap Music Promote Violence?

Rap musician Sean "Diddy" Combs leaves the court building after being found innocent on charges of gun possession and bribery.

Viewpoint

1

Some Rap Music Causes People to Be Violent

R.H. Aly

"Children should not be encouraged to join gangs."

In the following viewpoint R.H. Aly argues that rap music encourages violence and gang membership. Aly points to the glorification of gang activity in rap lyrics, as well as the actual gang membership of some rappers, as causes of children joining gangs. Aly is a former editor at the *Lantern*, a community newspaper for Ohio State University and surrounding areas.

AS YOU READ, CONSIDER THE FOLLOWING QUESTIONS:
1. Why does some rap music cause children to join gangs, according to Aly?
2. What famous rapper does the author point to as glorifying gang violence?
3. According to the author, how does gang membership affect rap artists' fame?

R.H. Aly, "Popular Rap Encourages Gangs," *Lantern,* June 2, 2003. Reproduced by permission of The Ohio State Lantern and the author.

Sometimes, I wonder why young children who couldn't be more than 13 or 14 years old would want to join a gang. I see the boundaries so clearly—a life of crime compared to a life of opportunity. It's almost as easy as seeing the difference between night and day.

"But if the line is so visible, why can't these children see it?" I ask myself. I often ponder if these youngsters know the benefit of an education and receiving a degree. Just one choice can be the difference between a life behind bars and a life fulfilling all of an individual's dreams.

The Lure of Gangs

Then, one afternoon, I came to a realization or at least part of the solution: These children saw success in hanging with gangs. They saw lots of Benjamin Franklins and Andrew Jacksons floating their way.

However, what made the dangerous, enticing gang pathway more enticing was the glory associated with—or what they thought to be glory. After all, some of the most famous celebrities are gangsters, and these celebrities are even proud of their gang associations.

One prime example is Calvin "Snoop Dogg" Broadus, the infamous rapper. Broadus prides himself on being a Crip, one of the most notorious gangs in Los Angeles. . . . The court commotion which occurred [in 1995–1996] was actually the consequence of a gang shooting. Broadus's bodyguard had shot an opposition gang member, and Broadus was caught in the middle of the trial. He even had to miss the MTV Awards because he was trying to avoid the clutches of the police. Later on, he turned himself in.

> **FAST FACT**
>
> According to a 2004 survey, most young people agree with the the statement, "Rap music videos have too many references to violence." Young women and girls (70 percent) are more likely than young men and boys (59 percent) to agree with the statement.

Even with all the criminal charges he was facing, Broadus still had his fans, and his fellow gang members loved the excitement. They probably thought it didn't really matter if one of the consequences was prison, because the iron bars just meant more fame.

Rap Lyrics Promote Violence and Gangs

To make things worse, the lyrics Broadus sings are not only riddled with cuss words, but the words also send violent messages to his fans. Instead of spreading such hateful messages, why couldn't Broadus try to send some life learning messages through his songs. Broadus isn't the only culprit. There's also Tracy Marrow (Ice-T), whose songs include "Street Killer" and "Where the S— Goes Down."

It's interesting these rappers think they're becoming role models to the children. They need to remember the risks. Tupac Shakur may have risen to fame, but his murder came about because of gang involvement. Notorious BIG is another celebrated gang member/rapper whose death helps portray the threatening menacement of gang practice.

Gang Membership, 1996–2005

Estimated Total Gang Membership Percentage Difference from the 10-Year Average of 750,000

Taken from: National Youth Gang Center. www.iir.com/NYGC/nygsa/measuring_the_extent_of_gang_problems.htm.

Tupac Shakur, injured in a 1994 gang-related shooting, was killed in another shooting two years later.

It's true both Snoop Dogg and Ice-T are rich, and they probably could have whatever they want by making one phone call, but there is no point in praising gang life. The lyrics in their songs won't stop children from wanting to join gangs. Instead, it will do the opposite. It will egg them on.

I'm not saying all rap music is awful, and no one should listen to the disgusting and dreadful music. There is still rap music I listen to, but I like the songs which are supposed to evoke meaningful lessons to every individual. I have to admit, I'm a big of fan of Eminem's music, where I see him making a big effort in trying to put some meaning into his songs—they're not all just about killing, drugs and sex.

Will Smith is another great rapper. While songs such as "Getting Jiggy with It" or "Men in Black," are not very mind stimulating (or in other words, they are not the kind of songs that could change a person's outlook on life) they are also not filled with abomination or loathing.

Children should not be encouraged to join gangs. Life is filled with so many opportunities. If they just took the chance, and bypassed the gang road, there could be so many windows which will open for them. It's certainly better than having some stray bullet end a person's life prematurely.

EVALUATING THE AUTHOR'S ARGUMENTS:

In this viewpoint R.H. Aly claims that rapper gang involvement and lyrics that celebrate gang violence cause children to join gangs. Do you agree? Why or why not?

Rap Music Does Not Cause People to Be Violent

Yaambo Barrett

"It is not the music one listens to that creates a certain type of person."

In the following viewpoint Yaambo Barrett argues that rap music does not cause people to be violent. Barrett claims that the reason rap music is often targeted as the cause of violence, instead of other forms of music, is due to racism against the largely black audience of rap music. Barrett believes that people have free will and choose to be violent, whether or not they listen to rap music. Yaambo Barrett is a graduate of Media Minds, a program designed to teach students twenty-first-century skills using the media.

AS YOU READ, CONSIDER THE FOLLOWING QUESTIONS:

1. Why does the author think that rap music is blamed as a cause of violence?
2. What does the author think would happen to violent crime rates if rap music is eliminated?
3. If rap music causes violence, what result would one expect to see from listening to "positive" music, according to Barrett?

Yaambo Barrett, "Rap Is Not the Bullet," *Media Minds Youth Mag*, November 2005. Reproduced by permission.

any people believe that there is a connection between the hip-hop music that is an integral social component of my generation and violence that exists in urban communities. However, I believe rap music has little to no correlation with violence. This is true for the following reasons: no conclusive causal relationship has been found between rap and violence; vilification of rap music is an extension of racism; and, most of all, human beings have free will and personal responsibility.

No Causal Relationship

If rap is to be indicted for its content, it must be compared equally to other art forms. Rap music videos and songs do not directly affect the mode of people's thinking in a manner that would make people resort to violence. People who commit crimes listen to numerous forms of music. Who is to say that it is rap music that influences people to act

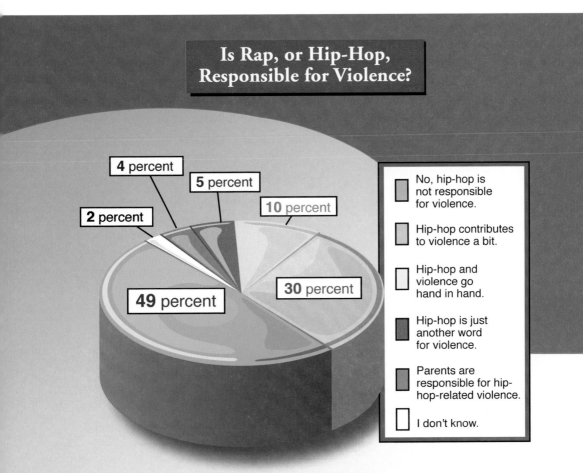

Is Rap, or Hip-Hop, Responsible for Violence?

- 4 percent
- 5 percent
- 10 percent
- 2 percent
- 49 percent
- 30 percent

- No, hip-hop is not responsible for violence.
- Hip-hop contributes to violence a bit.
- Hip-hop and violence go hand in hand.
- Hip-hop is just another word for violence.
- Parents are responsible for hip-hop-related violence.
- I don't know.

Taken from: About.com Poll. http://rap.about.com/b/a/258020.htm.

in a violent manner? The same person who listens to rap that commits a crime could also listen to rock and roll or techno as well. The research that currently exists does not demonstrate a causal relationship between rap and violence (meaning that if someone listens to a G-Unit song about committing murder, then a person will commit murder). However, many in the media choose to make the argument that rap causes violence. There is no basis behind the argument. This claim just seems like the PC (politically correct) thing to say because other forms of music do not contain the same type of intensity that is a part of rap. Just because rap is more aggressive does not mean that a cause and effect relationship exists. The argument that rap music causes violence runs deeper than simply the effect of music on the human psyche. It is an argument that deals with racial prejudice. The perception is that the majority of people who listen to rap music are black. If there is any increase in the rate of violence by black people it would be convenient to use the genre of music that a large number of black people, especially black youth, listen to as the scapegoat. Focusing in on rap music is similar to the historical stereotypes perpetrated in the media of black men as violent individuals. For example, the images contained in the movie *Birth of a Nation* were used to demonize blacks and sweeping indictments of rap are used in much the same fashion.

Fast Fact

A 2006 survey of college students was unable to establish any causal relationship between listening to certain music and ensuing violence or substance use.

People Have Free Will

There is no way to substantiate the claim that rap music causes violence. I do not believe that if rap were eliminated from the musical landscape today there would be a decline in violent crime rates. Music does not affect people that directly. Hearing a song about violence in the streets or about what another person has done doesn't make other people go out and imitate these actions. If a person thinks that rap causes violence they are using false logic. It is like saying that listening to "positive" rap music or classical music caus-

Jay-Z boycotted Cristal champagne after accusing the company president of making racist comments when he admitted that he wasn't thrilled with the brand's association with hip-hop culture.

es people to act in a socially conscious manner. Human beings act of their own free will. Consider this: it is not the music one listens to that creates a certain type of person. Music does not shape personality, as people may think. Rather, it may be the person's values and beliefs that make them choose the type of music they want to hear. I listen to rap and consider myself a fan. I hear shots; I've seen fights break out and been a part of them. I've seen drugs sold and seen guns drawn. Even though all this is true, like most people I have never acted out the violence contained in rap music. I, like most people, am in control of the choices I make, regardless of the music I listen to.

EVALUATING THE AUTHORS' ARGUMENTS:

In this viewpoint Yaambo Barrett argues that rap music is not the cause of violence. What would Barrett say to the previous viewpoint's author, Aly, regarding the claim that rappers are role models to children?

Rap Music Glorifies and Creates a Culture of Violence

"A lot of good kids are striving to conform to images established by clowns like 50 Cent and Snoop Dogg."

Bob Herbert

In the following viewpoint Bob Herbert argues that rap music celebrates violence and leads to young people embracing the values of rap music. This culture of violence, he says, has led to many tragedies, especially within the black community. Herbert calls on people, especially leaders in the black community, to work to change this culture of violence. Bob Herbert is an op-ed columnist for the *New York Times,* and his column is syndicated in other newspapers.

AS YOU READ, CONSIDER THE FOLLOWING QUESTIONS:

1. What are some examples Herbert gives of activities that are promoted by the values system of gangsta rap culture?
2. What example does Herbert give in support of his suggestion that there is a failure of black leadership on the violence issue?
3. What does the author say is the first step to changing the violent gangsta rap culture?

E dwin "E.J." Duncan was a young man from a decent family who spent a great deal of time with his friends in an amateur recording studio his parents had set up for him in the basement of their home in the Dorchester [Boston area] neighborhood.

It was in that studio that Duncan, along with three of his closest friends, was murdered last week [December 13, 2005], shot to death by a killer or killers who have yet to be found. Whoever carried out the executions, it seems clear enough to me that young Duncan and his friends were among the latest victims of the profoundly self-destructive cultural influences that have spread like a cancer through much of the black community and beyond.

The Need for Black Leadership

I keep wondering when leaders of eminence will step forward and declare, unambiguously, that enough is enough, as they did in the heyday of the civil rights movement, when the enemy was white racism. It is time to blow the whistle on the nitwits who have so successfully promoted a values system that embraces murder, drug-dealing, gang membership, misogyny, child abandonment and a sense of self so diseased that it teaches children to view the men in their orbit as niggaz and the women as hoes.

However this madness developed, it's time to bring it to an end.

I noticed that Jesse Jackson, Al Sharpton, Louis Farrakhan, Snoop Dogg and other "leaders" and celebrities turned out in South Central Los Angeles on [December 20, 2005] for the funeral of Stanley "Tookie" Williams, the convicted killer and co-founder of the Crips street gang who was executed in California [on December 13, 2005].

I remember talking over the years to parents in Los Angeles and elsewhere who were petrified that their children would be killed in cold blood—summarily executed, without any possibility of a defense or an appeal—by the Crips or some other gang because

Rapper Snoop Dogg, a former Crips gang member, protests the execution of Stanley "Tookie" Williams, Crips founder turned antigang activist.

they just happened to be wearing the wrong color cap or jacket or whatever.

The enthusiastic turnout at Tookie Williams's funeral tells you much of what you need to know about the current state of black leadership in the U.S.

The Influence of Rap

The slaughter of E.J. Duncan, who was 21, and his friends—Jason Bachiller, 21; Jihad Chankhour, 22; and Christopher Vieira, 19—was all but literally accompanied by a hip-hop soundtrack. Duncan, Bachiller and Vieira were members of a rap group called Graveside, which favored the rough language and violent imagery that has enthralled so many youngsters and bolstered the bottom lines of major entertainment companies.

This mindless celebration of violence, the essence of gangsta rap, is a reflection of the nihilism that has taken root in one neighborhood after another over the past few decades, destroying many, many lives. The authorities here have not suggested that Duncan or his friends were involved in any criminal behavior. But the appeal of the hip-hop environment is strong, and a lot of good kids are striving to conform to images established by clowns like 50 Cent and Snoop Dogg.

FOLLOWING in 50 CENT'S FOOTSTEPS...

The members of Graveside wanted badly to make it as rappers. Said one police officer, "They probably didn't even know they were playing with fire."

The Rev. Eugene Rivers, who has been fighting for years to reduce youth violence in Boston and elsewhere, was a neighbor of E.J. Duncan's. "My son Malcolm knew E.J. well," he told me. He described the murders as a massacre and said he has long been worried about the glorification of violence and antisocial behavior. "Thug life," he said, "is now being globalized," thanks to the powerful marketing influence of international corporations.

A Call to Action

This problem is not limited to the black community. E.J. Duncan and his friends came from a variety of ethnic backgrounds. But it is primarily a black problem, and it is impossible to overstate its dimensions.

I understand that jobs are hard to come by for many people, and that many schools are substandard, and that racial discrimination is still widespread. But those are not good reasons for committing cultural suicide.

I'll paraphrase [singer/songwriter] Sam Cooke: A change has got to come. Reasonable standards of behavior that include real respect for life, learning and the law have to be re-established in those segments of the black community where chaos now reigns.

This has to start with a commitment to protect and nurture all of the community's children. That may seem at the moment like a task worthy of Sisyphus [mythological king cursed to roll a huge boulder up a hill for eternity] because it will require overcoming what the Rev. Rivers has described as "the sins of the fathers who have cursed their sons by their abandonment and neglect."

Sisyphean or not, it's a job that has to be done.

EVALUATING THE AUTHOR'S ARGUMENTS:

In this viewpoint Bob Herbert suggests that gangsta rap celebrates violence in a way that perpetuates it. Do you think that getting rid of rap music that celebrates violence will reduce the amount of violence within the culture, or that rap music will cease to celebrate violence once the culture is less violent, or both?

Rap Music Is a Reaction to Violence in Society

Andrew Gumbel

"Rap as a whole was largely a response to the grim social conditions...."

In the following viewpoint Andrew Gumbel argues that rap music should not be blamed for violence. Rather, rap music should be understood as a reaction to the violence in society, Gumbel argues. He points to numerous examples of rappers who have been involved in violent activities, suggesting that their music merely reflects what was going on in their lives. Andrew Gumbel is a U.S. correspondent for the *Independent,* a London newspaper.

AS YOU READ, CONSIDER THE FOLLOWING QUESTIONS:
1. Why did Suge Knight, head of Tha Row records, end up in jail?
2. What two rappers' murders remain unsolved?
3. What conditions in the 1980s does Gumbel suggest as the source of gangsta rap?

A nyone trying to trace links between hip hop music and gun violence will inevitably look at the United States, where street killings, drive-by shootings, violent rap lyrics and the murders of three prominent hip hop stars have provided fodder for headline writers over the past 15 years.

Violence and Rappers

Many of the issues swirling in the aftermath of the New Year [2003] shootings of Latisha Shakespeare and Charlene Ellis have already had an exhaustive airing on this side of the Atlantic. Politicians, led by Tipper Gore, the wife of the former Vice-President Al Gore, have campaigned for years to clean up rap lyrics and restrict children's access to explicit material which, they say, encourages the climate of violence. Like Kim Howells, Ms Gore has been accused of everything from racism to reactionary cultural censorship.

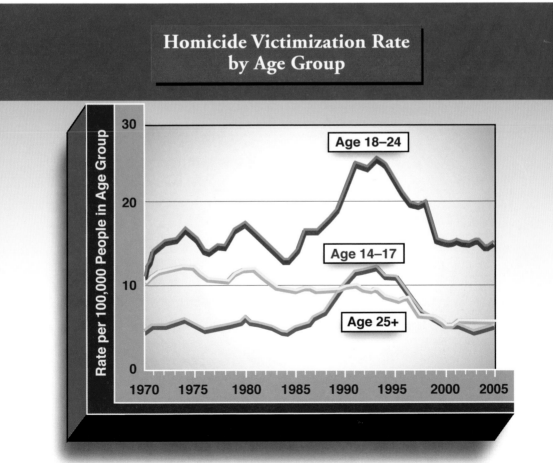

Homicide Victimization Rate by Age Group

Taken from: U.S. Department of Justice, 2006. www.ojp.usdoj.gov/bjs/glance/homage.htm.

The police and FBI have launched countless investigations into possible links between the moguls and DJs who create the most violent strains of hip hop music and the shootings of some of their closest friends and associates.

The feds raided the Manhattan offices of Murder Inc, a luridly named record label responsible for such stars as Ashanti and Ja Rule, in a search for evidence possibly linking the outfit to a notorious New York drug gang whose leader grew up in the same neighbourhood as Murder Inc's founder, Irv Gotti.

Police in Los Angeles rearrested the gangsta rap entrepreneur Suge Knight and threw him into jail on a parole violation after a year-long investigation into shootings involving employees and associates of Mr Knight's company, Tha Row (formerly known as Death Row Records).

It was Death Row which, in the early Nineties, spawned such acts as Snoop Dogg, who was charged and acquitted of a murder, and Tupac Shakur, who was shot and robbed in the lobby of a New York recording studio in 1993 and three years later, shot to death while driving in Mr Knight's car in Las Vegas. At the same time, Death Row became legendary for stories of intimidation, beatings and general thuggishness, stories that fell somewhere between reality and the deliberate macho posturing that is part of rap's public appeal.

> **FAST FACT**
>
> According to the surgeon general, male youths commit more violent acts than female youths.

Tupac's murder was followed three months later by the killing of one of his East Coast rivals, the Notorious B.I.G. Both crimes remain unsolved, and both remain the object of endless conspiracy theories involving East Coast–West Coast rivalries in the music business, gang showdowns between the LA Crips and Bloods, possible police corruption and more.

Last October [2002], Jam Master Jay, MC of the seminal Eighties rap group Run DMC, was shot dead in New York. His killing, which seemed particularly shocking since he had nothing to do with glamorising violence in his work, is also unsolved.

Death Row Records, cofounded by Marion "Suge" Knight, has been linked to gangs and some of the most controversial "gangsta" rappers.

Rap Is a Response

In the United States, gangsta rap grew out of a desperate inner-city culture in the Eighties marked by the explosion of crack cocaine use, the widespread availability of handguns (particularly the so-called Saturday Night Special) and the growing marginalisation of young black men excluded from the "greed is good" ethos of the Reagan era.

There may be some analogies to the spread of cocaine and illegal firearms in Britain today.

Rap as a whole was largely a response to the grim social conditions, not a spur to violence in itself. Clearly, though, there were links between criminality and the music business, at least at the margins. Much police energy has been spent looking for evidence of drug money being laundered through record companies, an endeavour that has so far made as little headway as the various murder investigations.

The Rappers with Attitude
Public Enemy

Attitude to women and guns: Flavor Flav was arrested for charges of assaulting his girlfriend in 1991. In 1993, he was charged with attempted murder for allegedly shooting at a Brooklyn neighbour.

Lyrics: From Yo! Bum Rush The Show: "Come on, let's step to the back, ya know what I'm sayin', I'll take you to the back and show you some of my techniques, and I'll stop a mud hold in your ass bitch. . . ."

NWA (Niggaz With Attitude)

Attitude to women and guns: Songs such as Find 'Em F— 'Em And Flee and To Kill A Hooker are violent. The album, *Efil4zaggin* had gang rape, paedophilia, cop killing, oral sex and prostitution.

Lyrics: From Straight Outta Compton: "Crazy motherf—er named Ice Cube, from the gang called Niggaz With Attitudes, when I'm called off, I got a sawed-off, squeeze the trigger, and bodies are hauled off, you too, boy, if ya f— with me, the police are gonna hafta come and get me off yo ass. . . ."

2Pac

Attitude to women and guns: Tupac Amaru Shakur had been arrested eight times by the age of 20, and served eight months for sex abuse. He survived being shot five times in a robbery in 1994. In 1996, Shakur, then 25, was shot dead after watching a boxing match with Death Row Records' president Marion "Suge" Knight.

Lyrics: From Secretz Of War: "War Time War Time, it's either yourz or mine Outlawz be on a grind, and a mission to shine And ride on em', leave em' stuck and f—ed from the gate. . . ."

Snoop Doggy Dogg

Attitude to women and guns: Calvin Broadus was arrested twice for gun possession after Long Beach Polytechnic High School. In 1993, he was acquitted of a drive-by murder. His first album, *Doggystyle* in 1993 caused rows over lyrics said to be violent and sexist.

Lyrics: From Gin And Juice 2: ". . . Cup of that Gin and Juice, I blank a bitch out, then turn the bitch out, look here, there ain't no need for you to be wastin' my time, see I picked you up, now I'm gunna stick you up, and dick you up!"

So Solid Crew

Attitude to women and guns: The group have made headlines for inciting gun culture with their lyrics and band members have been arrested on gun charges. In March [2002], Ashley Walters, aka Asher D, was sentenced to 18-months' detention at a young offenders' institution for having a loaded handgun. He was released in October [2002].

Lyrics: From Ride Wit Us: "This is my life, and still you're f—ing with me, telling you niggas, talking bout' you wanna blaze me. I am prepared for you. . . ."

EVALUATING THE AUTHORS' ARGUMENTS:

In this viewpoint Andrew Gumbel gives several examples of rappers involved in violent activities, whose music reflects that violence. Do you agree that the music is largely a reflection of violent conditions in society? What do you think the previous viewpoint's author, Herbert, would say?

Facts About Rap Music

Editor's note: These facts can be used in reports or papers to reinforce or add credibility when making important points or claims.

General Information
- The folk poets (called "griots") of West Africa have told stories rhythmically, accompanied by drums and other instrumentation, for centuries.
- In the 1970s deejays were "toasting," talking or chanting along with dubbed Jamaican dancehall and reggae music. Also in the 1970s jazz music artists were mixing jazz and poetry.
- In the 1980s rap music became more widespread, with rap artists such as Kurtis Blow, Run-DMC, LL Cool J, Public Enemy, Salt-N-Pepa, and the Beastie Boys gaining widespread popularity.
- Rap music is similar to many types of poetry in its use of alliteration, double entendres, metaphors, and similes.
- While only about 13 percent of the United States' population is black, according to the U.S. Census Bureau in 2005, almost all popular rappers are black.
- While most popular in the United States, rap is popular all over the world, with rap artists originating from numerous countries including Iraq, Tanzania, France, and Great Britain.

Types of Rap Music
- *Freestyle* rap usually denotes a type of rap where the lyrics are improvised.
- *Battle* rapping, which is often freestyle, refers to rapping competition between two or more rappers, usually in front of an audience.
- *Gangsta* rap refers to a type of rap about street life, with explicit lyrics about prostitution and crime. Gangsta rap became very popular in the 1990s with artists such as N.W.A., Ice-T, Tupac Shakur, and Snoop Doggy Dogg.

- *Conscious* rap is a term used to designate rap that strives to create awareness about social and political issues. It is further distinguished from the rest of rap by its aversion to violence, misogyny, and materialism.
- *Hip-hop* is a term used to refer to a cultural movement that encompasses music, dancing (breakdancing, in particular), DJing, MCing, and other art (notably, graffiti art). "Hip-hop music" is usually used interchangeably with "rap music."

Rap Music Consumption
- In 2003 Music Reports, Inc. (MRI) reported that 70 percent of rap consumers were white. In 2004, using a new method of gathering data, MRI found that 60 percent of rap consumers were white.
- According to the Recording Industry Association of America, hip-hop and rap music officially became more popular than country music for the first time in America in 2001.
- In 2006 rap sold 59.1 million albums.
- In 2006, for the first time in five years, no rap albums were among the year's ten biggest sellers.

Rap Music in Popular Culture
- Howard University, a historically black university, first offered a course in hip-hop in 1991. It now offers a minor in hip-hop studies.
- Many African American intellectuals, such as Princeton University professor Cornel West, are hip-hop fans. West, a well-known intellectual, made his own rap and poetry album, *Sketches of My Culture*, released in 2001.
- Former Public Enemy front man Chuck D has a political talk show, *On the Real*, on Air America Radio.

Organizations to Contact

The editors have compiled the following list of organizations concerned with the issues debated in this book. The descriptions are derived from materials provided by the organizations. All have publications or information available for interested readers. The list was compiled on the date of publication of the present volume; the information provided here may change. Be aware that many organizations take several weeks or longer to respond to inquiries, so allow as much time as possible.

Black Girls Rock
e-mail: info@blackgirlsrock.com
www.blackgirlsrockininc.com

The purpose of the Black Girls Rock organization is to combat the psychological effects of the disproportionate number of negative images of black women depicted in the media and make a difference in the lives of young women of color who are most affected by this imagery. The organization offers a mentoring outreach program and offers support through discussion, education, counseling, internships, mentoring, and advocacy.

Hip-Hop Association (H2A)
PO Box 1181
New York, NY 10035
(212) 500-5970
e-mail: info@hiphopassociation.org
www.hiphopassociation.org

H2A is a nonprofit community building organization that aims to utilize hip-hop culture to facilitate critical thinking and foster social change and unity by empowering communities through the use of media, technology, education, and leadership development. Focusing on the initiatives of media and education, it offers resources and news.

Hip-Hop Summit Action Network (HSAN)
e-mail: info@hsan.org
www.hsan.org

HSAN is a nonprofit, nonpartisan national coalition of hip-hop artists, entertainment industry leaders, education advocates, civil rights proponents, and youth leaders united in the belief that hip-hop is an influential agent for social change, which must be responsibly and proactively utilized to fight the war on poverty and injustice. The organization sponsors "summits," meetings to engage the hip-hop generation in community-building dialogues.

Just Think
39 Mesa St., Suite 106
San Franciso, CA 94129
(415) 561-2900
e-mail: think@justthink.org
www.justthink.org

Just Think develops and delivers curricula and innovative programs to build skills in critical thinking and creative media production. Their Web site contains media guides, alternative media, and other youth resources to encourage critical thought about different forms of media, including music and music videos.

Media Matters
The American Academy of Pediatrics
141 Northwest Point Blvd.
Elk Grove Village, IL 60007-1098
e-mail: mediamatters@aap.org
www.aap.org/advocacy/mediamatters.htm

Media Matters is a national public education campaign established by the American Academy of Pediatrics (AAP) to help pediatricians, parents, and children become more aware of the influence that media, such as popular music, have on child and adolescent health. The AAP publishes educational materials on the topic of youth and media.

National Association for the Advancement of Colored People (NAACP)
4805 Mt. Hope Dr.
Baltimore, MD 21215
(877) 622-2798
e-mail: youth@naacpnet.org
www.naacp.org

The NAACP works to ensure the political, educational, social, and economic equality of rights of all persons and to eliminate racial hatred and racial discrimination. The organization publishes numerous materials focusing primarily on the issues facing minority groups.

National Political Congress of Black Women (NCBW)
1224 W St. SE, Suite 200
Washington, DC 20020
(202) 678-6788
e-mail: info@nationalcongressbw.org
www.nationalcongressbw.org

The NCBW is a nonprofit organization dedicated to the educational, political, economic, and cultural development of African American women and their families. The organization gives testimony to political bodies, such as Congress, and publishes this testimony on their Web site.

Rap Sessions
PO Box 450832
Westlake, OH 44145
(440) 779-9893
e-mail: bakhannkru@aol.com
www.rapsessions.org

Rap Sessions organizes community dialogues on hip-hop. With a focus on the issues of gender and hip-hop and race and hip-hop, their Web site contains materials on these topics, including videos of discussions among academics, writers, and other members of the hip-hop community.

Take Back the Music Campaign (TBTM)
e-mail: takebackthemusic@essence.com
www.essence.com/essence/takebackthemusic

The TBTM campaign sponsored by *Essence* magazine was launched to raise awareness about the imbalance in popular culture's depiction of black women's sexuality and character. Encouraging readers to examine their views on the issue, it promotes artists that deliver positive alternatives to popular media. It publishes articles on the topic of women and rap, or hip-hop, music.

For Further Reading

Books

Jeff Chang, *Can't Stop Won't Stop: A History of the Hip-Hop Generation.* New York: Picador, 2005. Provides a history of hip-hop, with an emphasis on how the music has been shaped by history and culture.

———, *Total Chaos: The Art and Aesthetics of Hip-Hop.* New York: Basic Civitas, 2007. Includes essays, interviews, and panel discussions presenting views of hip-hop from key figures, scholars, and journalists.

Michael Eric Dyson, *Know What I Mean?* New York: Perseus, 2007. The author, a University of Pennsylvania professor, explores the controversies within the world of hip-hop, including the commercialism of the genre, gender relations, and other political elements.

Kenji Jasper and Ytasha Womack, eds. *Beats, Rhymes, & Life: What We Love and Hate About Hip-Hop.* New York: Harlem Moon, 2007. This collection contains essays on hip-hop culture, each of which focuses on a particular symbol of the genre.

Cheryl L. Keyes, *Rap Music and Street Consciousness.* Champaign: University of Illinois Press, 2004. Presents a history of rap, from its roots in West African bardic traditions, Jamaican dancehall, and African American vernacular expressions to its entry into the cultural mainstream.

Bakari Kitwana, *The Hip-Hop Generation: Young Blacks and the Crisis in African American Culture.* New York: Basic Civitas, 2003. An exploration of the disproportionate troubles black youths face and a discussion of how hip-hop may provide a solution.

———, *Why White Kids Love Hip-Hop: Wankstas, Wiggers, Wannabes and the New Reality of Race in America.* New York: Basic Civitas, 2006. The author examines the issue of race in America through an exploration of the popularity of hip-hop among youth of many races.

Tayannah Lee McQuillar, *When Rap Music Had a Conscience.* New York: Thunder's Mouth, 2007. Argues that rap music from 1987–1996 was used to inspire positive social change unlike the materialistic, violent, and sexualized rap music of today.

Joan Morgan, *When Chickenheads Come Home to Roost: A Hip-Hop Feminist Breaks It Down.* New York: Simon & Schuster, 2000. The author, an award-winning journalist and self-proclaimed "hip-hop feminist," discusses the issues facing African American women.

Richard Oliver and Tim Leffel. *Hip-Hop, Inc.: Success Strategies of the Rap Moguls.* New York: Thunder's Mouth, 2007. Provides an overview of how the rap music business evolved, with a focus on how wealth was created by the industry.

Imani Perry, *Prophets of the Hood: Politics and Poetics in Hip-Hop.* Durham, NC: Duke University Press, 2004. The author, a professor of law at Rutgers University, considers the art, politics, and culture of hip-hop through an analysis of song lyrics, arguing that hip-hop is first and foremost black American music.

Gwendolyn D. Pough, *Check It While I Wreck It: Black Womanhood, Hip-Hop Culture, and the Public Sphere.* Lebanon, NH: Northeastern University Press, 2004. In an exploration of the complex relationship between black women, hip-hop, and feminism, the author discusses the influence of prominent female rappers.

Gwendolyn D. Pough, Elaine Richardson, Aisha Durham, and Rachel Raimist, eds. *Home Girls Make Some Noise! Hip-Hop Feminism Anthology.* Mira Loma, CA: Parker, 2007. Presents a collection of essays that challenges the view of hip-hop as a "male space," identifying the ways women have been involved in the culture from the beginning.

Tracy Sharpley-Whiting, *Pimps Up, Ho's Down: Young Black Women, Hip-Hop and the New Gender Politics.* New York: New York University Press, 2007. Explores the complicated relationship between young black women and hip-hop culture, including rap music.

S. Craig Watkins, *Hip Hop Matters: Politics, Pop Culture, and the Struggle for the Soul of a Movement.* Boston: Beacon, 2006. The author explores the hip-hop movement, identifying challenges of the movement, including the corporate takeover of hip-hop and the rampant misogyny in rap music.

Periodicals

Kimberly L. Allers, "The New Hustle: More Rappers Are Moving from Lyrics and Videos to Booming New Business Ventures. But Too Many Have Figured Out the Quickest Route to Riches Is

Pimping 'Hos' and 'Bitches.' A Look at the Buying and Selling of Hip-Hop," *Essence,* August 2005.

Shilpa Banerji, "Life After Imus: The Debate Has Already Begun over Whether Hip-Hop Culture Perpetuates the Denigration of Black Women," *Diverse Issues in Higher Education,* May 3, 2007.

Martha Bayles, "Heedful Hip Hop," *Wall Street Journal,* April 28, 2005.

David Brooks, "Gangsta Rap en Français," *International Herald Tribune,* November 11, 2005.

James Clingman, "Elistist Hip-Hopcrisy," *Black Voice News Online,* June 21, 2007. www.blackvoicenews.com.

Davey D., "Who Let the Dogs Out? Blame It on Hip-Hop," August 2, 2007. www.ballerstatus.com.

Globe and Mail, "Time to Talk About Violence and Culture," December 29, 2005.

Tommy Gorman, "Is Hip-Hop Music Getting a Bad Rap?" *Daily Aztec,* February 16, 2005.

Hip-Hop Summit Action Network, "Recommendation to the Recording and Broadcast Industries: A Statement by Russell Simmons and Dr. Benjamin Chavis on Behalf of the Hip-Hop Summit Action Network," April 23, 2007. www.hsan.org.

Bakari Kitwana, "The Cotton Club: Black-Conscious Hip-Hop Deals with an Overwhelmingly White Live Audience," *Village Voice,* June 24, 2005.

————, "Hip-Hop Slang Spreads Wrong Word: The Jargon Behind Imus' Dispute Is Prompted by Financial Greed, but Both Races Should Rethink Its Toxic Cultural Message," *Newsday,* April 13, 2007.

David Lowery, "Hip Hop Hell: Lessons a Father Can Learn on a Long Ride Home," *Austin American-Statesman,* June 19, 2004.

John McWhorter, "Rap Only Ruins," *New York Post,* August 10, 2003.

Bryan Monroe, "From the Message to the Conversation: Why Black America's Self-Examination Needs to Go Beyond Hip-Hop and Get Real," *Ebony,* July 2007.

New York Post, "Programming Killers," December 1, 2005.

Shelly Palmer, "The Rap on Freedom of Speech," *Huffington Post,* April 27, 2007. www.huffingtonpost.com.

Edward Rhymes, "Caucasian Please! America's True Double Standard for Misogyny and Racism," *Black Agenda Report,* April 18, 2007. www.blackagendareport.com.

Adrienne P. Samuels, "Russell Simmons—the Godfather Takes a Stand," *Ebony,* July 2007.

San Francisco Chronicle, "Rapping Up Those Words," May 20, 2007.

T. Denean Sharpley-Whiting, "'Pimpin' Ain't Easy: Hip-Hop's Relationship to Young Women Is Complicated, Varied and Helping to Shape a New Black Gender Politics," *Colorlines Magazine,* May/June 2007.

Brent Staples, "The Hip-Hop Media—a World Where Crime Really Pays," *New York Times,* June 8, 2005.

Rachel E. Sullivan, "Rap and Race: It's Got a Nice Beat, but What About the Message?" *Journal of Black Studies,* May 2003.

Carla Thompson, "Hip Hop Women Recount Abuse at Their Own Risk," *Women's eNews,* June 11, 2006. www.womensenews.org.

Carol Walker, "Hip-Hop Culture Crosses Social Barriers: Musical Artists Tell America's Story in Rap," May 13, 2006. www.usinfo.state.gov.

Diane Weathers, "The Message in Our Music," *Essence,* June 2004.

Dana Williams, "Hip Hop's Bad Rap?" *Tolerance.org,* February 23, 2003. www.tolerance.org.

Susan Young, "Artists Help Move Hip-Hop Beyond Misogyny, Violence," *Oakland Tribune,* February 20, 2007.

Web Sites

Baller Status (www.ballerstatus.com). This Web site has rap music news, editorials, videos, blogs, and links to other sources.

Consciousrap.org (www.consciousrap.org). This Web site has a showcase of conscious rap videos and links to articles on conscious rap.

Index

Picture Credits

Maury Aaseng, 18, 25, 29, 35, 42, 55, 61, 66, 73, 77, 87

AP Images, 10, 20, 23, 30, 57, 74, 79, 83, 89

Brad Barket/Getty Images, 68

Raymond Boyd/Getty Images, 49

Robert Mecea/Getty Images, 70

Alexander Sibaja/Getty Images, 62

M. Szwajkos/Getty Images, 44

Mario Tama/Getty Images, 34

Ray Tamarra/Getty Images, 39

Alex Wong/Getty Images, 13